The Garden Guy

A Seasonal Guide to Organic Gardening in the Desert Southwest

by

David Owens

The Garden Guy –
A Seasonal Guide to Organic Gardening in the Desert Southwest

For more information address: Poco Verde Landscape,
520 West Warner Road, Tempe, AZ 85284.

FIRST PRINTING: May 2002

Library of Congress Cataloging in Publication Data
ISBN: 0-9705016-1-7

The GardenGuy® is the registered trademark of David Owens
and the property of Poco Verde Landscape, Inc.

Published and Distributed by Poco Verde Landscape.

Cover photo credit: Keith Farnham
Research/editing: Jennifer Warren
Book design/layout: Joann Kotyk, Composing Arts, Inc.

Printed in the U.S.A.

Contents

Also by David Owens:

EXTREME GARDENING

How To Grow Organic In The Hostile Deserts

Introduction

When looking at your garden, think of it as an extension of your home. Your garden is a series of different types of rooms with focal points and themes in each area. These areas could be composed of plants and trees that attract butterflies and birds and surround a small patio, to an area containing a barbecue, and table and chairs. This all could be underneath a wood or steel arbor allowing shade during our intense summers. The possibilities are endless.

This book gives you a month-by-month guide on approaching these projects and many more, from a natural, organic point of view. Look at your garden as a mini eco-system that will attract many types of visitors, human and animal alike.

Your garden will open up an entirely new vista for you and the more you learn from nature, the more you will understand the natural systems that take place.

One of the most important elements to keep in mind is to avoid using synthetic pesticides, herbicides and fertilizers in your eco-system. Also, try to understand how to create that natural balance that Mother Nature has been using for billions of years.

Basic Steps

... To Organic Gardening

- *Allow your grass clippings to return to the soil.*

- *Avoid using synthetic fertilizers and pesticides.*

- *Begin using compost, natural fertilizers and volcanic rock powders.*

- *For specific problems use pesticides that are natural or least toxic.*

- *Plant at the proper time of year and use native, well-adapted plants.*

- *Mulch is a must for all bare soil.*

- *Water less often but deep and thorough when you do.*

January

Calendar for Organic Gardening

Water
- Deeply and infrequently.

Prune
- Remove dead or damaged limbs from shade trees.
- Trim flowering trees but twigs no larger than pencil size. Evergreen shrubs also, if needed.
- Best time for fruit trees is late winter before bud break.

Fertilize
- Rye lawns.
- Beds of asparagus with manure based fertilizer late in the month.

Pest Control
- Watch for aphids.
- Houseplants: Spray with liquid seaweed, mild soap, and biostimulant mixture to control mealy bugs, scale, and spider mites.

Plant
- Containerized trees, shrubs and vines.
- Bare root roses.
- Berries, grapes, asparagus, onions, English peas, fruit and pecan trees, anemones and ranunculus.
- Early in the month finish tulip and daffodil plantings.
- Vegetable seeds and spring flowers indoors.

- Mild weather allows for flowering kale, cabbage, pansies and dianthus.
- Plant bare root fruit trees. Make sure they are the low chill varieties.

Odds 'n Ends

- Remove winter weeds.
- Harvest citrus.
- Keep compost pile moist; turn monthly or more often.
- Plan for your spring landscape improvements.
- Add compost and volcanic rock to your garden soil.
- Add mulch to bare soil.
- Don't forget to have your mower serviced and all your tools repaired before Spring!

January

Companion Planting

Life is no fun without friends. They keep us out of trouble when we're headed the wrong way, help us in times of need and give us a reason to enjoy life. This is also true with plants. Certain plants do better together than they would when planted separately.

I have found when landscaping and planting gardens, there are relationships between plants that we don't understand, but when planted together, certain plants thrive in an environment that they normally would never grow in. These types of companion plantings are called communities. These communities, or poly-cultures, are composed of symbiotic plant relationships that help prevent disease, repel insects and sometimes help take care of each other's fertilizer needs. As I have said before, we don't fully understand all of the benefits of companion planting, but we do know it has been practiced for thousands of years and it's dangerously close to becoming a lost art.

Believe it or not, it's spring in the desert already and that means if you are planning on getting started on a garden, now is the time to do it. Companion planting is the only way to go and I can give you a few essentials on this type of gardening.

No garden should be without the following three basic crops, which are good companions for almost everything and are easy to grow.

Lavender is one of my favorites, especially Lavandula multifida. It grows in well-drained soil and has a pleasant scent, which helps ward off insects. It also attracts pollinators to its flowers, which in turn help pollinate the plants that depend on pollination for fruit production.

Nasturtium is another type of plant to companion plant with almost anything. They flower and are edible. They are delicious in salads and on sandwiches with a little cream cheese, but the best thing about them is that they work as a trap crop. A trap crop is a crop that we sacrifice to the insect gods in order to keep the insects away from our primary crops. Try it. You might like it as much as the insects do.

Last but not least, is to companion plant so that the plant is helping out other nearby neighbors. One such plant is the *legume.* These plants belong to the pea family and are able to fix nitrogen through symbiotic relationships with nitrogen-fixing bacteria in soil. They are the workhorses of our gardens. Every garden in the world should have at least one good neighbor called Mr. and Mrs. Legume.

Suggestions On Companion Planting

Lettuce; *plant with:*
Radishes

Eggplant; *plant with:*
Lavender
Marigold
Tansy
Wormwood
Thyme

Tomatoes; *plant with:*
Basil
Sage
Asparagus
Peas
Marigolds
Nasturtium
Chamomile

Radishes; *plant with:*
Squash
Cucumber
Peas
Lettuce
Nasturtium
Tea leaves

Deciduous Fruit Trees

This is a good time of year to plant deciduous fruit trees or bare-root fruit trees, such as peaches, apricots, plums, figs and apples. I recommend the following varieties:

Peaches: Desert Gold and Mid-Pride
Apricots: Royal Blenheim, Gold Kist, Katy
Plums: Santa Rosa, Beauty, Laroda
Figs: Black Mission and Conadria
Apples: Ein Sheimer and Anna

Many nurseries sell nectarine trees, but they do not grow well in the valley.

When you're ready to purchase trees, ask a nursery for low-chill hour deciduous fruit trees. Low-chill hour refers to the number of hours it is between 36 degrees and 48 degrees. The above-mentioned trees need between 100 and 300 hours.

Don't buy flowering or leafing trees because these trees have already used up their reserve energies needed for a healthy root system.

Soak 2 to 5 hours in water before putting the trees in the ground.

Put them in the ground as soon as possible.

Plant on a low-lying area with a northern exposure.

Preferably, you don't want the trees to get sun during the winter. Sun cuts down the number of chill hours.

Cut back the branches so the tree remains low to the ground. This makes it easier to cover the tree with a net to guard against birds.

Plants And Trees That Produce Edible Fruit

Many times when landscaping, we forget that our plants can be grown for the food that they can produce. Right now is a great time to purchase and plant these trees and vines as bare root. You cannot produce a safer or healthier organic food product than fruits and berries off of your own trees and vines.

I know there are pundits out there that will tell you it is impossible to grow your own, but mark my words, it's easy and inexpensive, especially when you are going to use the plants and trees that are already part of your landscaping.

One of my favorite types of fruit is the blackberry. Blackberries do extremely well in the valley, but you need to do a couple of things. The first is to pick the right types. Womack, Brazos and Brisons are the three types that do best here in the valley. Each has its own individual characteristics that may be superior to the other. You can get the full details in my first book, ***Extreme Gardening.***

You must make sure to plant the blackberries in an area that gets afternoon shade and has plenty of room for the plants to spread. I have friends that actually grow these as an income crop.

Figs are another one of my favorite types of trees to grow. Black Mission and Conadria seem to thrive here in the valley. Make sure to plant them in a warm, frost-free area.

Plant them where the roots receive plenty of water during the first few years, and make sure to keep a lot of compost around the base of the trees. This helps with its fertilizing needs and also retains the moisture.

Peach trees are normally short-lived, lasting from 10 to 15 years on average. These trees are increasingly easy to grow. A few varieties are Desert Gold, Babcock and Florida Prince. Make sure to go with the types that require low-chill hours to produce fruit. You also need to keep them relatively short so the tree can be covered with netting to keep the birds away from the fruit.

Some other types of trees easily grown in the Valley are:

Apples: *Anna, Golden Dorsett, Ein Sheimer*
Apricots: *Gold Kist, Katy, Royal Rosa, Blenheim*
Plums: *Santa Rosa (best tree for the desert), Gulf Gold, Gulf Ruby*
Pomegranates: *Wonderful!*
Persimmons

Be sure to purchase the above named trees to get the best results. When purchasing these trees, keep in mind you need early-bearing, low-chill trees to have a successful fruit-bearing season.

Insect-Repelling Plants

There are a lot of plants to start planting in your garden, but there are a few that do a great job repelling insects.

I surround my vegetable garden with upright rosemary. It not only repels insects, but it looks good as a hedge. You might want to try the trailing rosemary as a ground cover. Both have a dark green color and look good contrasting with the light grays of artemisia or santolina, which also work as great insect distracters. You might want to try artemisia around roses, especially Gene Boerner or Pink Simplicity. Both have pink flowers and look beautiful with the light green of artemisia.

If you have dogs or cats, you might want to grow catnip in the runs. It has a tendency to be a little invasive, but it repels fleas and ants. You might want to try growing it in pots around your pets' feeding bowls. Some other plants to try are tansy and rue, which repel fleas. You can plant lavender to keep ticks away. Remember, lavender needs very well drained soil here in the Southwest, so mix a lot of sand into the hole when you plant it.

If you are having problems with ants, try sprinkling bay leaves throughout your pantry and cabinets. Bay trees are easy to grow and no garden should be without one. Bay trees are also known to repel moths. You might want to try tansy, peppermint and geraniums. All have been known to ward off ants.

One last herb that I grow almost all year-round is basil. I have some basil in my garden that has been there for more than two years. It can be grown in the ground and in pots to ward off flies and mosquitoes. It is frost-tender, so try covering it in low temperatures. Keep it pinched back for bushy growth. Don't be afraid to add a little to your pasta.

Permaculture Gardening

If you're tired of digging up hard soil to garden in, only to find poor results, you might want to try permaculture gardening. I have had amazing results with it.

First, select an area about 4 feet by 10 feet. Cover the area with blood meal. Add 6 to 10 inches of compost.

Next, put down 1/4 inch of newspaper and water the entire area. On top of the newspaper, lay 6 to 10 inches of straw and water the area again. You'll end up with a raised bed.

Now, you're ready to plant. Small plants, such as broccoli, cauliflower and tomato plants work great this time of year. Cut holes in the newspaper and plant them right into the straw, leaving the plants level with the top of the straw.

Backfill with compost and water every 2 to 3 days in the winter and once daily in the summer.

The following year, build another garden on top of the old one. The old one will decompose.

Pruning

Pruning is a necessary element of landscaping and here in the desert, it is critical that pruning take place over the next few weeks. Pruning is one of the most confusing and difficult tasks to teach and do here in the Southwest. It could be considered more of an art than a science.

Grapes are one of my favorite plants to grow here in the desert. I normally use them to shade my garden during the summer and because they are dormant during the winter, the vines allow for light to warm my garden during the winter. The biggest confusion about grapes is how to prune them. Normally, if you are trying to optimize production, you need to prune them in certain ways.

Types of pruning needs include:

> *Thompson Seedless - cane pruning*
> *Perlette - spur pruning*
> *Flames - spur pruning*

Cane pruning is basically removing everything but 2 to 3 canes along a central leader.

Spur pruning is removing all of the growth except 8 to 20 small spurs along a central leader. Your best bet is to sign up for a class or learn from a neighbor.

With trees, make sure to thin out any dead or dying wood and prune out any cross branches or any branches that don't create a 45 degree angle from the trunk of the tree. Don't skip pruning your stone fruit trees such as peaches, plums and apricots.

A couple of rules for pruning include:

- *Use the correct tools.*
- *On most trees, with the exception of peaches, never prune more than 1/3 of the plant or tree.*
- *Most plants need to be pruned right after their flowing cycle.*
- *Never prune below the collar of the main trunk.*
- *If you are not sure, get advice.*

The Right Soil For A Healthy Vegetable Garden

You can plant vegetables any time of the year as long as the soil temperature is right. Here are the correct temperatures for several vegetables:

Asparagus	-	50 to 60 degrees
Beans	-	60 to 70 degrees
Beets	-	40 to 50 degrees
Cabbage	-	40 to 50 degrees
Carrots	-	40 to 50 degrees
Cauliflower	-	40 to 50 degrees
Swiss chard	-	40 to 50 degrees
Corn	-	50 to 60 degrees
Cucumber	-	60 to 70 degrees
Eggplant	-	60 to 70 degrees
Lettuce	-	35 to 45 degrees
Onion	-	35 to 45 degrees
Peas	-	40 to 50 degrees
Peppers	-	60 to 70 degrees
Pumpkin	-	60 to 70 degrees
Radish	-	40 to 50 degrees
Spinach	-	35 to 40 degrees
Squash	-	60 to 70 degrees
Tomatoes	-	50 to 60 degrees
Turnips	-	40 to 50 degrees
Watermelon	-	60 to 70 degrees

To ensure you have a healthy garden, you can do one of two things. The first method is to put in a 4 foot wide garden, making sure you leave paths 2 feet wide to get a wheelbarrow through. Use a Rain Bird T-tape to water the garden.

The other way is to dig a trench that is 2 feet deep and 2 by 4 feet wide. Fill it with one bag of manure and then backfill with the dirt you dug up.

Additional amendments you might want to integrate into your garden to make it healthier are soft phosphate, blood meal, soil sulfur and compost, along with an application of my Extreme Juice, which is a favorite of mine. Always look for quick-maturing fruits and vegetables because the valley has very short seasons. Plants that mature in 60 to 80 days are ideal.

Here are some vegetables you can plant right now:

Artichokes
Asparagus
Beets
Cabbage
Carrots
Collard Greens
Kale
Lettuce
Mustard
Onion sets
Parsley
Peppers *(Protect from frost)*
Spinach
Tomatoes *(Sweet, Celebrity, Early Girl are good - Protect from frost)*
Turnips

To increase soil temperatures, use plastic. You can build a small plastic greenhouse with PVC pipe (good for tomatoes) or with concrete wire mesh and plastic over small trenches approximately 3 to 4 inches deep with soil mounted up on both sides (works well with broccoli and swiss chard). These are all great ways to increase soil temperatures and get a quick start on a vegetable garden and be able to grow during the cool months.

Tune-Up Time For Your Roses

Get out those sharpened and clean pruning shears because in the next 2 to 4 weeks, you need to start pruning back your roses. There are three methods of pruning, depending on what type of roses you have. For tea roses and grandifloras, I like to prune back approximately 1/3 to 2/3 of the rose and be certain you prune to an outward-facing bud eye. I like to prune the rose back to 5 to 8 canes each 8 to 12 inches long. Remember to remove several of the oldest stems and leave a lot of the mid-size stems. The rule of thumb is that the larger and sturdier the stem, the larger the flower. The smaller the stem, the smaller the flower.

For floribundas, shrub roses and polyanthas, shear back the roses by 1/3 to 2/3. Remove or thin out any dead wood and strip off all the leaves. This should be done on all roses no matter what kind they are.

For cane roses, prune off the 3 to 5 year old canes and remove any dead wood. Remember to cover all your cuts, 1/2 inch or larger, with lipstick or Elmer's glue to prevent insects and pathogens from entering.

Once you're finished, make sure you spray your roses with a dormant oil spray. I make my own with 1/4 to 1/3 cup vegetable oil and 1 tsp. soap per gallon of water. This kills all those nasty bugs that may be trying to play snowbird on your leaves.

Turf Grass Care

If you're thinking about your lawn right now, you're probably not alone, especially when watching Phoenix Open golfers hit those 300-plus-yard drives down beautiful lush fairways at the TPC in Scottsdale.

But I can guarantee this golf course is not like a lot of others here in the valley. They have made a concerted effort to go as nontoxic as possible when maintaining the course.

Lawns are probably the largest contributors to air pollution, chemical runoff and pesticide/herbicide contamination than any other single item in your home, including your automobile. If you recognize this and want to do something about it, think organic.

Organic types of fertilizers and pesticides are a lot easier on our environment and safer for your pets and small children. Both synthetic fertilizers and pesticides have been proven to contain dangerous amounts of deadly chemicals that could contribute to long-term health consequences and environmental damage.

Let's first talk about fertilizers. Most of our summer grasses are a hybridized Bermuda type and during the winter, a perennial rye. Your major macronutrient requirement is nitrogen.

During the summer for iron and nitrogen, I use bat guano, Texas Greensand, blood meal, Gardenville 6-2-2 and Gardenville 7-2-2. For small lawns, I recommend coffee grounds or cottonseed meal, most at a rate of 20 pounds per 100 square feet. I'll start backing off on the nitrogen in late July or early August and start using a chelated iron or Texas Greensand.

By the time winter rolls around, it is rye grass season. This is really the season of outdoor living and the finest time of year to have a great lawn. If it were up to me, I would ban Bermuda grass lawns because they are water hogs and besides that, who uses a lawn when it's 120 degrees outside?

In the last 10 years, I have noticed that rye grass lawns have held on well into June. I start overseeding in September, so there will only be 3 to 4 months of Bermuda hell, which takes up a tremendous amount of our personal and environmental resources.

Perennial rye grass lawns should be overseeded in late September to early November and top-dressed with 1/4 to 1/2 inch of manure. Manure contains high amounts of nitrogen and a plethora of micronutrients. This application will usually get you through to middle to late December and you will have to switch over to blood meal, combined with applications of humic acids, from January to February, then back to cottonseed meal and Texas Greensand when the soil temperature starts increasing. Or try Extreme Juice in a foliar application.

As for pesticides, I do occasionally dose my lawn with beneficial nematodes, which help with my grub, tick and flea problem and diatomaceous earth if my cricket or ant problem gets out of hand. But that's it. Remember, I concentrate on my winter lawn as my primary crop. Good blends of perennial rye grass that contain high doses of naturally occurring endophytes like Repel, Citation II, Pennant, All Star and Prelude will take care of your bug problem. Endophytes are a fungus that bugs find tastes bad and naturally don't want to be around. As for herbicides, I find it distasteful that someone would take it upon themselves to spray a weed killer and contaminate our environment to avoid looking at a weed.

Let's go over my weed-fighting strategy. First, grow rye grass. It's allopathic and fights weeds naturally. No one should put in a lawn that is not overseeded like I said previously. I would encourage all of us to change our paradigm and let our summer grass go dormant and treat our winter lawn as our primary lawn.

Next, pull your weeds before they flower. If you followed my advice so far, you probably don't have many weeds, but don't let your weeds go to seed. Every weed represents seven years worth of work. The third thing to remember is use only natural products to eliminate weeds. Spray your weeds with straight vinegar or try a pre-emergent called WOW at *www.gardensalive.com.* It is a by-product of corn that naturally kills weed seed in our soil and it's safe for kids and pets. Along with all of those benefits, as it breaks down, it fertilizes your lawn. For spot treatment, try Gardenville Natural Weed Control.

Grapes, Asparagus And Blackberries

One of the easiest plants to grow has got to be grapes. Grapes are used for shade, as well as fruit. I have even seen folks use the grape leaves for cooking.

I normally purchase bare root grapes in early January and plant them on a western exposure. Be sure to add a lot of compost and soft phosphate to the hole before planting.

Trellises are usually necessary, and I use concrete reinforcement wire attached to the structure.

Over the next 6 to 8 months, with plenty of water, this plant will burst with tons of growth. This growth needs to be trimmed back in the winter, to one trunk that will form the main trunk of the future plant. When this trunk gets 2 to 3 feet off the ground, cut the top off. A couple of shoots will develop from this shoot, which will now be used to grow parallel to the ground and then up the trellis. It's an experiment of sorts, and you'll find the vines are very forgiving.

As the vines get older, you will need to start pruning your grapes back. This will maximize fruit production. Depending on the type of grape you plant will determine the pruning method.

All grapes need to be pruned severely after the training period, which is normally 3 to 4 years. Pruning takes place in January and you normally take off anywhere from 80 to 90 percent of the growth that formed on the first 3 to 4 years of base growth. As for specifics to pruning, you need to probably visit one of the local nurseries to get more details.

When buying grapes, nothing beats Thompson Seedless for hardiness. Thompsons' produce in August and a few vines will produce more grapes than you can use. A couple of other varieties you might want to try are Muscat and Flame. Make sure to protect your harvest from marauders like birds by taking small paper sacks and inserting the grapes into the bag and stapling it at the top.

The only fertilization application you need to worry about is in May or June. Use an organic fertilizer such as dairy cow manure, bat guano or Rocket Fuel. A zinc application may be necessary too. Make sure that your vines are well irrigated up until harvest and then you can cut back after you have reaped your harvest from the vine.

As for pests, the worst by far is the grape leaf skeletonizer. This little varmint can wreak more havoc on your grape vines than a bull in a china shop. Your first clue that this guy is coming to visit will be when you see a little black moth, approximately 1/2 an inch long, flying among your vines. Believe me, he is not there to sight see. The second clue is the eggs will hatch and produce a black and yellow caterpillar on the underside of the leaves. These caterpillars will start eating your leaves, leaving the basic structure of the leaf with no green showing. When you see it you will know exactly what I mean.

To control these guys, kill the moth and search the underside of the leaves and look for pinhead sized eggs or the caterpillar and rub them out with a gloved hand. Or you can try spraying bacillus thuringiensis (BT). Be aggressive and you will win, but if you wait too long your vine will disappear.

Asparagus grows great in the valley and will last 30 to 100 years. Use them as backdrops to flower beds. You can buy them right now. Make sure you plant them in afternoon shade. For fast results, plant them approximately 12 to 15 inches apart in a bed approximately two deep. Fill the hole halfway up with 1/2 compost and 1/2 soil. Backfill it halfway with the compost/soil mixture. Put in the roots and cover them up with 2 to 3 inches of soil.

As they grow, continue to backfill with the compost/soil mixture. Wait until the leaves die back next winter and cut back. Continue this process and in approximately 3 years, you'll start having spears.

Start harvesting in three years by snapping the spears off at ground level once they reach 8 inches tall. After 4 to 6 weeks, stop picking and allow the rest of the stalks to grow out and mature over the summer months. This will revitalize the root system so they can produce another crop.

Fertilize moderately in the springtime with Extreme Juice.

Blackberries are another great fruit to grow in the Southwestern desert. Plant them in afternoon shade. Try Brazo or Womack. They are highly invasive, so you must plant them in 15 gallon buckets. This will restrain the root system from growing outside its boundaries. Trellis against a wall or fence for easier picking.

You can buy them at most nurseries or mail order them.

January Notes:

February

Calendar for Organic Gardening

Water
- Deeply and infrequently.

Prune
- Roses.
- Remove dead, diseased and cross limbs from your shade and ornamental trees.
- Foliage with winter damage, if danger of frost is over.
- Grapes 80 to 90 percent, peaches and plums 40 to 50 percent to encourage 45 degree angle growth. Pecan trees need little or no trimming. Do other fruit trees as needed.

Fertilize
- Citrus, roses, lawns, grapes and deciduous fruit trees.
- With a natural fertilizer to all planting areas.
- Use worm castings, fish meal and bat guano for cool season flowers (10 lbs./1,000 sq. ft.).
- Spray Extreme Juice on growing plants and flowers.

Pest Control
- To help control grub worms, fire ants, fleas and other pests apply beneficial nematodes.
- For serious infestations of scale insects use horticultural oil. Make sure to keep mixture shaken while using.

Plant

- Annual color.
- Blackberries and fruit trees.
- Glads, cannas, daylilies, alyssum, calendulas, snapdragons, petunias and pansies.
- Onions, asparagus, English peas, cauliflower, cabbage, broccoli, brussel sprouts and other cold tolerant vegetables.

Odds 'n Ends

- Repair and adjust sprinkler system.
- Turn compost pile.
- For all unhealthy soil areas add a top-dressing of mulch and compost.
- Repair gardening equipment for spring use. Don't forget to sharpen mower blades, hoes and pruning tools.

February

Beneficial Insects

We need to change our self-reliance on synthetic pesticides and fertilizers and let Mother Nature take over. If you knew how toxic the chemicals in synthetic pesticides and fertilizers were, you would be shocked.

It's so easy (and good for you and the environment) to go the natural way. The idea of releasing beneficial insects as an alternative to using pesticides is an inexpensive, effective way to keep your garden naturally balanced.

A great way to control several problems in your garden is with insects. Here are uses for a few of my favorite multi-legged creatures:

Lacewings: They feed on moths, aphids, thrips, mites, mealy bugs, scale and whiteflies. Lacewing eggs are sold in small containers of sawdust and should be dusted around your garden. They are also sold as live insects.

Dragonflies: These little guys do a great job of controlling mosquitoes, horseflies and gnats. In fact, they can eat 300 to 400 pesky insects each day. Dragonflies are attracted to birdbaths and other small areas of standing water. They occur naturally in our environment.

Trichogramma Wasps: These wasps are actually small and cannot sting, so there's no need to worry about getting stung. At any rate, they have an appetite for all kinds of bad guys in your garden, so give these beneficial bugs a try.

Other insects to consider:

Big-Eyed Bugs
Lady Beetles/Ladybugs
Praying Mantids

If you'd like to purchase a few beneficial bugs, you should check out *www.buenabiosystems.com.*

Note: *I have even limited my use of natural pesticides by growing nectar-producing flowers. By encouraging beneficial insects with these types of flowers, I strike a balance between good insects and pests. This limits the use of any pest control that might upset the bio-diversity and balance we're trying to achieve in and around our home.*

Fertilizing

It's getting to be that time of year to start thinking about fertilizing your trees, roses, vegetables and other plants around your yard. There are a few things you should keep in mind when fertilizing with inorganic fertilizers. Typically, synthetic fertilizers cause quick, succulent growth that is more susceptible to disease and insect damage, and contaminate our ground water supplies. You also kill a lot of beneficial organisms in the soil that help plants manufacture food, which helps your plants and lawn grow.

The Environmental Working Group *(ewg.org)* said that synthetic fertilizers contain chemical waste, comprised of compounds, cadmium, mercury and other known carcinogens. Synthetics also do not add carbon to your soil which is needed to create microbiotic activity, which is the starting point to having a great garden.

If I were going to have only one item to help my garden grow, it would be compost. Good compost not only fertilizes, but also reduces water consumption and disease. I top-dress my rose beds, vegetable garden and lawn with compost, gradually reducing any extra fertilizer needed during the year. Spread 2 to 4 inches of compost around your shrubs and trees but do not let the compost come in contact with the trunks. Be sure to spread the compost out to the drip line of the plant or tree.

In addition to compost, other natural fertilizers include:

Cottonseed Meal: *great lawn fertilizer for Arizona.*
Fish Emulsion: *good in the garden and for outdoor plants. Use it as a foliar feed to build strong healthy plants and repel insects. For indoor or outdoor plants, use a dash of molasses to curb odor.*
Liquid Seaweed: *good as a disease fighter (available at all Fry's Market-places) and repels white flies and spider mites. It contains trace elements and acts as a chelating agent, making other fertilizers and nutrients more available to the plants.*

Epsom salts can be used for roses and daffodils and help produce bigger canes and brighter blooms. Use 1/8 to 1/4 cup around each rose bush. Put about 1 tsp. around each daffodil bulb and try making a foliar spray of 1/4 cup to a gallon of water and spraying it on your roses.

You might try something unconventional and place coffee grounds, which are full of nitrogen, around your plants. Add banana peels around your roses to help them resist insects such as aphids.

Remember, you are feeding the soil, not the plant. By using organic fertilizer, you are building up disease resistance, decreasing the amount of water needed and fertilizing your garden with natural products that don't harm the environment.

Great Garden Tools

When I do any project around my house or business, I want to make sure that my tools fit the needs of the job. It's important to use your tools for the purposes for which they were designed. Often, people will grab any old tool out of the shed to do their work, but that can cause problems. Using the wrong tool for the task can sometimes cause the job to take longer, require you to work harder and allow the end result to suffer.

Now, you wouldn't expect a watchmaker to use a pipe wrench, nor would you see a ditch digger using a tablespoon. I know these examples are a little extreme, but the principle is the same: *Choose the right tool for the job.* To help you with this edict, I've listed a few of my favorite gardening tools below.

Hula Hoe: This old-timer is a great way to get rid of weeds and unwanted grasses.

Dual-Blade Hoe: This is a new take on a classic. You can use this to slide back and forth for weeding or tearing out vines. But the real benefit of owning one of these babies is the angle of the blades. When planting seeds, use them to move soil to make a perfect furrow without having to bend over. Just stand, slide the soil over, drop the seeds and go!

Trenching Shovel: If you've got to dig a trench for a sprinkler system or if you're burying cable, a regular shovel will cause too much stress on your back. But the blade on this tool is long, narrow, sharp and angled perfectly to dig even trenches efficiently. I also use this tool to remove weeds.

Small-Headed Shovel: These are fine for some jobs, but to dig holes for planting, or other small tasks, a regular shovel makes you work harder for no good reason. But nothing breaks through our hard-packed soils like a pointed, small-headed shovel (4 to 6 inches wide).

Flat-Nosed Shovel: When you're moving fill dirt or spreading gravel, a flat-nosed shovel is the way to go.

Sharp Shooter: This tool is meant to help you dig into hard-packed soils. It's essentially a small-headed shovel with a lot of weight and beefed-up construction. The handle is extra long, usually metal and weighted so you can slam it down and break apart whatever you're digging into. This baby is so tough that it can break through cement. You can find it at irrigation supply stores.

Fruit Picker: Tried and true, this tool gets a lot of use at my place, collecting fruit that's too high for me to reach. At the end of a long pole, there's a little basket with a claw. Maneuver the basket around citrus or fruit, and give a tug. The claw pulls the fruit off the stem and the basket holds the fruit until you can get it to the breakfast table.

Soaker Hose: This hose is great for watering plants, grasses, and gardens and just about anything. It looks just like a regular black garden hose, except it has a lot of tiny holes around it that allows water to seep out and soak into the ground. By the way, a good addition to the hose is a mechanical timer that attaches to the hose spigot and does not need electricity.

Soil Probe: A soil probe allows you to determine whether or not you're watering your trees, gardens, shrubs and lawn deeply enough.

Have fun in the garden!

Healthy Soil

Often trees and plants start to decline for no reason, but remember it's not natural for trees or plants to be grown in a sterile environment. Many times trees and plants have different relationships with the micro flora and fauna that we do not completely understand, but we know these symbiotic types of relationships exist. Often, we unknowingly destroy these mutually beneficial relationships through the use of synthetic pesticides and fertilizers. The use of these types of poisons destroys our ecosystems and the natural balance that many plants use to survive our harsh environment. Because of this, it is necessary to rebuild these microenvironments around our trees and shrubs with natural fertilizers and fungicides, which build up the microbes.

The secret to fixing a sick tree or shrub is a matter of re-establishing the natural make up of the soil. The first thing to do is create an oxygen root exchange inside and outside of the drip line of the tree. This could be as simple as using a core aerator (the type used for lawns and readily available at most rental shops) and core aerate through the drip line area and beyond. Remember, most of the feeder roots are at the drip line. I also use a hand core apparatus and copper pipes with a high-pressure nozzle at the end, which when hooked onto a hose and forced into the soil creates an oxygen rich environment. All of these procedures will create well-oxygenized soil, as well as an environment where beneficial micro flora and micro fauna will thrive.

The second trick is to spread some sort of stimuli so the microbes have some reason to hang around. I put down approximately 5 pounds per 1,000 sq. ft. of dried and liquid horticultural molasses. Another good addition to your soil would be cornmeal at 20 pounds per 100 sq. ft. Cornmeal is a natural disease fighter that feeds the beneficial microbes in the soil and naturally fights fungus.

For a final treatment, cover your soil with 2 to 4 inches of compost. Compost is a natural fertilizer that helps cool the soil and retains moisture. It increases the porosity of the soil and actually cleans-up chemical damage and fights weeds. Make sure to install it out beyond the drip line of the tree or plant, and make sure it does not touch the base of your tree or plant.

Top-dress the soil with 4 to 6 inch native tree trimmings.

For extra measures foliar feed your trees with 1 cup of manure tea, 2 oz. of liquid seaweed and 1 gallon of water (or use my Extreme Juice). Foliar feeding is one of the best treatments you can use on a tree and goes a long way to the tree's overall appearance and longevity. Foliar spraying should be done during morning time. Do it in small amounts - often.

Insect-Repelling Herbs

Stop! Don't reach for those pesticides. Many times, insects end up controlling themselves, but did you know that some plants have insect-repelling qualities? I have picked out a few that will grow here in the valley and can be planted along with other plants as companion plantings.

Thyme: Works great with cabbage and likes to be grown in an area that receives afternoon shade. It repels cabbageworms and takes care of many of other insect pests that may be bothering your garden.

Tansy: No garden should go without tansy in it. I grow it in the shade with a little morning sun and it produces a yellow flower when in bloom. I use tansy as a deterrent around my home spreading the leaves on my patio, and making up a tea as a natural repellant.

Nasturtiums: These flowers are one of the easiest plants to grow from seeds and they spread out all over the garden. Their leaves and flowers are edible and they work great as a trap crop. What does a trap crop mean? Well, it's a plant that insects prefer over other plants when they are feeding. Nasturtiums work kind of like a plant decoy. Aphids, white flies and other bugs love to hang out in nasturtiums. You can also use Lantana as a trap crop for white flies.

Basil: This is one of the easiest plants to grow in a pot. It's edible, but it also wards off flies and mosquitoes, so try some around your outdoor cooking areas.

Lavender: One of the prettiest plants has got to be lavender. It's tall and spiky with purple flowers and gray foliage. It makes a great accent to any landscape. It holds up best when planted in well-drained soil. Because of its scent, lavender makes a great addition to any garden and it also repels ants. And, of course, don't forget garlic. It repels bores, beetles, aphids and spider mites. Don't forget that roses should not be planted without garlic growing underneath them.

Keep Your Flowers Fresh

Get ready, because it is time to buy those flowers for your sweetie. The old saying, *"You get what you pay for,"* is even truer when purchasing fresh flowers, especially with roses.

One question to ask before buying roses is how fresh are they? Usually florists have the freshest roses that have been picked within 48 to 72 hours. Also, look for roses that look like they are just opening. This indicates freshness and a good quality rose. Also look for firm buds. I also check the stems, looking for the freshest cut. The stems need to have 1/2 to 1 inch cut off one time per day. This is critical for flower longevity.

A great way to keep woody-stemmed flowers, like roses and carnations, alive is to immerse the stems in 100 to 110 degree water. I then put them in a cool, dry place out of direct sunlight. I do this with all fresh cut roses from my garden and it works for most cut flowers. The warm water forces open the stem tissues and helps the plant drink the water. You might also try making a vertical cut into the stem with a sharp knife. I make two cuts for safe measure and scrape the outer bark along the bottom inch or so. I then recut the stems and change the water every day, making sure the water is at least 100 to 110 degrees.

Hollow-stemmed plants are another story. Delphiniums, daffodils and chrysanthemums have hollow stems. I prick hollow-stemmed flowers with a sharp pin once at the top near the blossom. I then fill the stem with water and plug it with cotton or a small piece of paper.

For poppies and other flowers with milky fluid, I cauterize the ends of the stem with a torch or match. You can do this by holding the stem over a flame for 20 to 30 seconds.

To help with longevity, add 1/2 tsp. chlorine bleach to a can of regular 7UP™ and mix it in a bucket. Use this mixture to fill the vase. Another recipe is to mix 1 tbsp. sugar, 2 tbsp. lemon juice and 2 tbsp. bleach with a quart of water in a bucket and use in your vase.

Planting Season

Beans: Plant by seed through April 15th. Usually the bush varieties produce more quickly than the pole varieties. I suggest planting the asparagus, Chinese or long bean. This vine type veggie is fast growing, takes up a lot of space and is very prolific. Plant in a southern exposure and be prepared to pick beans often. They love hot weather.

Beets: These may still be planted by seed through March 15th. Choose an early-maturing variety or plant as "greens." Try Renee's Dutch Baby Ball Beets. Tiny and sweet, they are ready in about 55 days from seed. Plant beets and onions together.

Carrots: Plant by seed through April. Choose the short types for heavy clay soils. Consider the early-maturing varieties so they may be harvested before the high heat of summer. Prepare the soil deeply (8 to 12 inches) with organic material (but not fresh manure as this causes the carrots to develop hairy roots). Carrots are rich in calcium and phosphorus and make a satisfying snack any time. Plant carrots with peas, lettuce, chives, onions, rosemary, sage and tomatoes.

Corn: There is still time to get the spring corn crop in. Plant by seed through April 1st. Again, plant early-maturing varieties. Plant in blocks (4 to 5 rows by 4 to 5 rows) for effective pollination. Do not mix different varieties together or cross-pollination will occur and the corn will not be true to the varieties planted.

Cucumbers: Plant by seed through May 1st. Try the bush varieties (if space is tight) or grow the vining varieties up a trellis to save space.

Melons: Mid-February begins the melon-planting season. Cantaloupes and muskmelons may be seed-planted through the end of July. Melons enjoy enriched soil. Dig a large hole and amend with 50% compost. Mound the soil and plant several seeds on top. Thin to 2 vines after true leaves (at least 2 sets of leaves) appear. Keep the vines watered deeply.

Watermelons may be planted mid-February through the end of April. Plant as above. Try the smaller varieties unless there is a lot of room for the vines to spread. As fruits appear, lift them off the ground to prevent rot and minimize insect damage. Place the fruits on a thick layer of straw, boards or even foam board from home improvement centers. Try Sugar Baby which was developed to fit easily into your refrigerator.

Peas: The sugar pod varieties of peas are especially delicious. Plant seed through February. Better yields are obtained by using an inoculant for peas and beans. Inoculants contain beneficial bacteria, which helps "fix" nitrogen in the air and makes it available to the plants.

Pumpkins: Plant pumpkins by seed in March. Follow the suggestions for growing melons. The next month to plant pumpkin seeds is July for Halloween jack-o-lanterns.

Radishes: Plant radishes by seed through April. These are wonderful for children to plant because they sprout so quickly. Radishes are available in many different varieties. Try some of each, especially the French Breakfast or White Icicle varieties.

Summer Squash: Plant summer squash by seed through April 15th. These squash will produce better if they are assisted with pollination. The male flower (usually first to appear, grows more upright and without the small bulb at its base) needs to be shaken over the female flower (with a small bulb at the base of the flower and usually not so upright). This pollination can also be done with a paintbrush. Collect the male flower pollen and brush it inside the female flower. Again, keep developing fruit off the soil with alfalfa hay or partially completed compost to prevent rot or insect damage.

Winter Squash: Plant winter squash by seed during the month of March. This vegetable requires a long growing season and usually needs a lot of space. The bush varieties produce more quickly and do not take up as much room.

Remedies For Getting Rid Of Pests

Our gardens attract a lot of critters, mostly good – but a few are bad. I constantly talk about how biodiversity is the key ingredient to our gardens, but sometimes rabbits, birds, dogs and cats want to use our garden as much as, if not more than, we do. It's a frustrating experience and one not easily rectified, but the Garden Guy is here with some new and not-so-new ideas on how to clean up the problem – organically of course.

Rabbits invariably find their way into our gardens, especially if you live in the outlying areas of the valley. They seem to come out of nowhere and in the dark of night. A good dog works great, but some other ideas that stop their appetite would be to liberally apply some bone meal and blood meal to the soil of the plants. They also seem to have an aversion to cayenne pepper, as do cats. If all else fails, try fencing material about 2 feet high and buried 6 inches into the soil. For rabbits I have also used Shake Away Rodent Repellant, human hair and drenched the soil with human urine.

I have had a tremendous amount of calls on how to get rid of gophers. These pesky critters have a way of tunneling in areas that are right where we find ourselves waiting to look at or play in. I consider myself an ace trapper, but the secret is leaving no human scent on the trap. I first purchase a gopher trap, which are found in most feed stores. I then boil the traps in water for 5 to 10 minutes with a stick of creosote and I make sure I handle them with gloves that are covered in plastic, assuring that no scent is left on the trap. You must find the lateral tunnels and set the trap so it lies parallel to the tunnel run.

Another idea is to use dry ice. Dry ice can be stuck into the mound entrances and covered up. Make sure to find and cover up all of the holes so that the gas does not escape. The carbon dioxide will slowly seep into all the runs and you don't want to know the rest of the story. I have also poured castor oil down the holes. Also, I have stuck road flares down the holes, spearmint chewing gum and Shake Away Rodent Repellant.

Dogs seem to be an ongoing problem and if they are anything like my dogs they like to dig. A solution to this problem that I have used in the past is to blend together one part cayenne pepper, two parts mustard powder and two parts flour. Apply wherever they dig or whatever else dogs do and they soon avoid these areas. If you have a dog that does not get the idea, try pure cayenne pepper.

As for cats, I will take clippings from the rose bushes – it needs to have a lot of thorns – and apply them to the areas they frequent, and I plant an herb called rue. Rue can also be rubbed on furniture to keep cats from scratching. Last, but not least, if those pesky pigeons are making your home their home, try a light spraying of Dr. Bonner's Peppermint Soap, which can be found at Wild Oats. A lot of times, this is more effective to spray while they are roosting.

Roses

We're getting to the end of rose-planting season and there are a few things you need to do to have beautiful, healthy roses.

Here are a few roses that grow well in the valley:

Don Juan: a climbing rose with the darkest red blooms I have ever seen
Gene Borner: a great bloomer, produces pink flowers
Showbiz: a shrub rose guaranteed to bloom without any work
Queen Elizabeth: large-blooming rose
Tropicana: produces beautiful colors
Ora Gold: one of the most beautiful yellow roses I've ever grown in the
   valley
Mr. Lincoln: a red tea rose just like the ones you buy at the florist

Shrub Roses:
   Red Simplicity: blooms all the time
   Pink Simplicity: blooms all the time
   Carefree Wonder: blooms in cycles

Some of my other favorite roses include:

Abraham Darby: nice blooms and fragrance
Othello: very fragrant
Marmalade Skies: blooms all the time
Fairy Rose: deer resistant
Collette: big thorns

As soon as you see new leaves, fertilize with a good rose food, preferably one that is organic, such as steer manure, cottonseed meal, fish emulsion, or Extreme Juice. Roses are high-nitrogen consumers and need a lot of fertilizer. To increase blooming, foliar feed one time per week during the blooming seasons and use Extreme Juice.

Onions and garlic make great companion plants for roses. Plant your roses next to the herbs to ward off pesky insects that will be prevalent later in the year. Banana peels, when worked into the soil, will repel insects.

Spring Flowers

Flowers That Like Shade

Begonias
Rain Lilies
   Yellow and white varieties go dormant in the summer, die back to the
      soil
   Pink varieties bloom in the late summer and stay evergreen
Geraniums
   Like afternoon shade
   Let dry between waterings
Iceland Poppies
   Vibrant against a light-colored wall
   Terrific with alyssum
Dianthus
   Edible
   Likes afternoon shade
   Fragrant varieties
   Likes company of other plants

Johnny-Jump-Ups
  Edible flowers
  Reseed readily
  Nice edging plant for shady areas

Flowers That Like Sun

Marigolds
Zinnias: partial shade is OK
Cosmos
Globe Amaranth
  Needs warm weather
  Everlasting and dries well
Tithonia: also known as the Mexican Sunflower
Verbena
Celosia
Salvias
Portulaca: also known as Moss Rose
Geraniums: Pelargoniums
  Drought tolerant
  Like dry soil between irrigations
  Plant with roses, corn and grapes
  Controls ants
  Plant on east side of yard with shade in afternoon
  Need well-drained soil
  3 to 4 inch cuttings root easily in a glass of water
  Fertilize regularly
  Frost tender
  Try cascading varieties over railings
Lavender
  Perennial shrub
  Cut the flower stems as the buds just begin to open
  Cut off the top 3 to 4 inches of the plant to rejuvenate after flowering
  The fragrance from the flowers and leaves helps you sleep
  Add clean and dry flowers to some honey, let sit for one week and then
    use as a delicious flavoring
  Needs well-drained soil
  The fragrance distracts moths, rabbits, mice and ticks

Bulbs

Plant with the following plants to help disguise the drying foliage:
Alyssum: reseeds readily
Thyme

Flowering Bedding Plants

Dig in 6 inches of compost 12 inches deep along with 5 pounds soft phosphate and 3 pounds of soil sulfur per 100 sq. ft. Raise bed for drainage. Rotate flowers and plants from year to year. Plant the dark and bright-colored flowers against a white wall. Plant light-colored flowers against dark walls. Remove dead flowers to encourage new growth.

Some Companion Plant Combinations:
Petunias
Annual
Cool-season flower
To encourage flowering, pinch off flower at least 1/2 inch beyond petals to remove seed-producing ovary
Periodic shearing, or dead heading, will rejuvenate plants and boost flowering
Fertilize every 2 weeks with fish emulsion or Extreme Juice
Cascading variety is great for hanging baskets
Water in the morning
Plant with lettuce, broccoli, beans, cauliflower and squash
Chrysanthemum Palludosum
Annual
White, daisy-like flower with yellow center
8 to 12 inches tall
Re-seeds readily
Disease and pest-free
Great companion plant for lettuce
Marigolds
Like sun
Soil needs to be 70 to 75 degrees for seed to germinate
Easily grown from seed
Wrap leaf around minor finger cuts
Brew flowers to create antiseptic tea
Edible flower petals
Attract hover-flies, a beneficial insect

Kill verticillium wilt in soil

Great companion plant for vincas

All marigolds originally from Central America

The gem series has a wonderful lemon scent

Control nematodes on roses, bulbs and strawberries, especially the Mexican Marigold

Nasturtiums

Good trap crop

Orange or yellow flowers ward off aphids

Edible flowers, leaves and seeds

Do not use pesticides on edibles

Direct plant 1 inch deep, where it will receive evening shade

Too much shade, too much water and too much nitrogen fertilizer will result in lots of leaves but no flowers

Tomatoes

Start planting tomatoes when the soil temperatures turn 50 degrees, which is about now. Tomatoes need three things: afternoon shade, a lot of compost mixed with soft phosphate, Texas Greensand and Volcanite (mix about 20 percent in the hole) and fertilizer (like Extreme Juice).

In Arizona, you need to buy short-season varieties of tomatoes. These will get you tomatoes in less than 60 to 70 days. I suggest buying Early Girl, Heat Wave, Sweet 100's, Better Boy or my favorite, Celebrity. It's my favorite because it's extremely disease-resistant.

Plant them on their sides to take advantage of warm soil temperatures. Make sure to remove any leaves below the soil line.

Consistent watering is crucial to grow tomatoes in the valley. You may want to bury a small coffee can right beside the tomato plant with holes in the sides and the top exposed. Fill the can up to water the tomato plant. This helps with deep watering. Or mulch with 4 to 6 inches of compost.

With as cool as the temperatures are right now, use a tomato cage and surround the tomato plant with clear plastic, creating a small greenhouse to protect it from cold winds. Make sure the plastic doesn't come into contact with the plant itself.

Fertilize every 2 weeks with fish emulsion, liquid seaweed, or Extreme Juice, which will help the plant resist frost damage. You can also fertilize with cottonseed meal or compost tea.

Tomatoes grow well beside companion plants. Choose nasturtiums (I like the Alaskan variety), onions, cosmos, asparagus, petunias, carrots, marigolds, parsley, alyssum and one of my favorites, basil.

Let your tomatoes grow into a thick bush. This will protect the plants from intense sunlight and increase humidity around the tomato plants.

As it gets hotter, remove the plastic and cover your tomatoes with cheesecloth.

Wait until the last minute to harvest the tomatoes. Let them stay on the vine as long as possible after they turn red and pick just before using.

If you're picking green tomatoes and you need them to ripen, combine them with bananas or apples and the gases the fruit give off will ripen the tomatoes.

Winter Gardening In The Low Desert

The trick to having an early and abundant harvest is to get those vegetables in the ground as early as possible. Here are some tips to help your winter garden flourish:

1. Plant early-maturing and short-season varieties for best results.

2. Use Wall O' Water to retain heat around the plants during the winter.

3. Use the new fabric mulches to warm the soil, retain water, increase yields and reduce pest and disease damage.

4. Use red fabric mulch (Selective Reflecting Mulch) with tomatoes and strawberries. SRM increases yields up to 20 percent.

5. Use gray-green fabric mulch (100 percent Infrared Transmitting Mulch) with heat-loving plants, such as melons, peppers, eggplants, squash and cucumbers. IRT 100 raises soil temperatures as much as 15 to 20 percent.

The fabric mulches and the Wall-O-Water can be ordered at **gardenguy.com**. Don't forget to protect the seeds from cold weather and birds.

Vegetable varieties to direct sow now include the following:

Beets *(smaller varieties mature much faster)*
Cabbage, broccoli, brussel sprouts and bok choy
Carrots *(short varieties)*
Lettuce and mescaline mixes

Green bunching onions, chives and parsley
Peas
Radishes
Spinach
Swiss chard
Direct-sow tomatoes
Turnips

These transplants can also be placed in the garden, but remember to protect them from the cold and birds:

Artichokes
Asparagus
Cabbage, broccoli, brussel sprouts, cauliflower and bok choy
Bunching onions, chives, garlic chives and parsley
Potatoes
Swiss chard
Tomatoes

February Notes:

_____

_____

_____

_____

_____

_____

_____

_____

_____

_____

_____

_____

_____

_____

_____

_____

_____

_____

_____

_____

March

Calendar for Organic Gardening

Water
- Deeply and infrequently.

Prune
- Your vines and spring flowering shrubs after they finish blooming.

Fertilize
- Use Extreme Juice to spray all growing plants.
- Use a natural organic mixture in all planting areas.

Pest control
- Aphids: Spray with hard streams of water; add 2 oz. molasses per gallon for better results. Release ladybugs and lacewings.
- Extreme Juice plus 1 cup skim milk per gallon of spray works for black spot, powdery mildew, and bacterial leaf spot.
- Dust around plants with a mixture of hot pepper, cedar flakes and natural diatomaceous earth for pill bugs, slugs and snails. Also use garlic-pepper tea and beer traps.
- For caterpillars, loopers and grape leaf skeletonizers use Bacillus thuringiensis biological work spray, then release trichogramma wasps.
- Fruit trees need to be sprayed with Extreme Juice plus garlic tea at bud break and again after flowers have fallen from the trees.

Plant

- Melons, squash, peppers, cucumber and corn.
- Shrubs, trees and citrus.
- Finish planting cool season annuals.
- After last killing freeze, start planting warm season crops and annuals.
- Your summer herbs: sage, oregano, mint, lavender, thyme, lemon verbena, salad burnet, lemongrass, etc.

Odds 'n Ends

- Thin fruit on deciduous trees.
- Spray Olive Stop on mulberries and olives.
- Remove frost damage.
- Add mulch to bare soil.
- Turn the compost pile.
- For bed preparation use completed compost.
- Shredded native tree trimmings or partially completed compost works well as a top-dressing mulch to keep the soil cool during the summer.

March

A Garden Without A Garden

No land? No space? Wrong sun exposure? Even without a plot of land, you may have a beautiful and productive garden grown entirely in containers.

Or you may simply wish to enhance your existing garden, patio or other outdoor living rooms by decorating with containers.

It's simple, it's easy and it's inexpensive, considering the potential for an explosive mass of vibrant color or vegetables right where you want them.

Remember, the summer heat will cause any container to dry out quickly, so be prepared to water often, daily if necessary.

The first step is to choose the container.

Purchase nothing smaller than the equivalent of a 5 gallon container.

Otherwise the soil will heat up too much in the summer and you'll end up "steaming" the roots when you water the plant.

Also, light-colored containers will keep the soil cooler than dark-colored pots.

Try foam pots. They have a higher insulating factor than either plastic or terra cotta pots.

Wooden barrels are another good choice.

For decorative containers without drainage holes, place a smaller pot inside, raised off the bottom with a brick or inverted saucer and plant in it.

For a unified, 3-D look, group three to five pots of varying sizes together.

Next, provide drainage. To do this, drill one 3/4 inch hole for every square foot of container bottom.

Add 1 to 2 inches of pea gravel or styrofoam beads and then put a piece of hardware fabric or screening on top of the gravel or styrofoam.

Lift the pots off the ground with bricks, pot feet (specially made to raise pots) or movable dollies. It's much easier to do this before the pots are filled with soil and plants.

Now add the soil. Use a commercial soil-less potting mix or try making your own for an inexpensive, fast-drying, nutrient-holding mix.

For a homemade recipe: mix 7 parts compost, 6 parts Volcanite, 5 parts worm castings, 4 parts Texas Greensand, 2 parts peat moss, 1 part rock phosphate, and 1 handful of aged steer manure.

Place the plants in the containers. Choose plants with similar sun or water requirements for each pot. Don't mix plants that have different sun or water needs.

When positioning the plants, allow 4 inches of clearance from the top of the root ball to the top of the pot to allow for a layer of mulch and for watering.

For color, plant densely. Place the tallest plant in the middle. The mature size of the plant should be no more than 1-1/2 times the height of the pot. Fill in around the central plant, including plants that will trail or drape over the edges of the container. A touch of white in any grouping will emphasize the colors of the other plants.

For vegetables, choose the bush or dwarf types. Look for the early-maturing varieties so they will produce more quickly. The climbing or vining type veggies may be grown up a trellis placed in the pot when the soil is added.

The following vegetables need 6 hours of sunlight daily: *(morning sun is crucial)*

Warm-weather crops:
> Patio or cherry tomatoes
> Peppers
> Melons
> Cucumbers
> Eggplants
> Beans
> Corn: if the containers are large enough and you put a grouping of pots together to speed up pollination.

Cool-weather crops:
> Lettuce
> Cabbage
> Broccoli
> Cauliflower
> Beets
> Carrots
> Spinach
> Peas

Herbs:
Many herbs lend themselves to pot culture. Tuck them in with both flowers and veggies. They will attract beneficial insects and repel the pesky ones.
> Marjoram
> Mint
> Basil
> Rosemary
> Thyme
> Summer Savory
> Sage
> Chives
> Marigolds
> Nasturtiums
> Parsley

Watering: Daily in the summer or when temperatures reach 90 degrees. 2 to 3 times a week in the fall and spring. 1 to 2 times a week in the winter.

Fertilization: Because of frequent watering, it's necessary to feed with a good organic fertilizer, such as fish emulsion, liquid seaweed or Extreme Juice, at least every two weeks or use a more diluted solution every time you water.

Liquid seaweed, which may be purchased at Fry's Marketplace, improves the heat and cold resistance of the plants.

Pest Control: Check plants often for insect damage. Don't forget to look on the undersides of the leaves.

For infestations of unwanted bugs, use Safer's insecticidal soap or a home-made solution of 1 to 2 tbsp. blue dishwashing liquid to 1 gallon of water.

For fungus gnats, which are harmless but irritating, drench the soil with B.T.I., available at *arbico.com,* or dust the soil surface with baking soda and let the top of the soil dry out between waterings.

Remember, the stronger the plants are and the more vigorous they grow, the fewer pest problems. Pests are attracted to weakened and stressed plants. And one last item, top-dress the soil with cedar bark.

The Battle Of The Bugs

With the warm weather on its way, our homes are going to get infested with insects. Here are some ways you can arm yourself in the battle of the bugs:

To ward off cockroaches, dust with diatomaceous earth along all baseboards and seal cracks. Inside you can dust with boric acid.

To kill wasps, fill a soda bottle about halfway with fruit juice and put old hamburger meat inside. The wasps will go in the bottle and drown.

To get rid of ants inside, make up traps of 9 parts peanut butter or sugar to 1 part boric acid. Place it on a piece of cardboard out of the way of children and pets. Your ants will be gone in 2 to 3 weeks.

To get rid of ticks, boil 20 eucalyptus leaves in 1/4 quart water for 10 minutes. Let cool and apply on pets or spray on your lawn. Dust lawn with diatomaceous earth.

To eliminate crickets, place a piece of dry dog food in the middle of a piece of duct tape and lay in the yard. Crickets will stick to the tape.

Apply a 50/50 solution of baking soda and water to a mosquito bite to stop the itch.

To control mosquito larvae, put a little instant coffee in birdbaths.

To eliminate most insects, use eucalyptus or cedar chips as mulch.

Citrus Trees In The Valley

Now that frost danger has passed, it's time to plant citrus.

Here are some tips:

Location: Choose an area as frost-free as possible. Choose tangerines and grapefruit if you live in a cooler area. Allow 20 feet minimum between each tree.

Rootstock: Look for sour orange, troyer or carrizo rootstocks. This information should be listed on the tree tag.

Planting: Dig the hole wide but only as deep as the root ball. Carefully set the plant in the hole. A broken root ball is a dead tree. Cut off the container if necessary. Backfill with the same soil that was removed from the hole.

Irrigation: Construct a berm under the drip line for irrigating. Water every three to five days to establish. Irrigate every 7 to 10 days in summer and 15 to 20 days in winter. Prevent water from sitting against trunks by constructing a second berm 6 to 12 inches away from the trunk of the tree.

Pruning: Every cut is a wound, so prune as little as possible. Protect the trunk of citrus with a mix of 50 percent white latex paint and 50 percent water or wrap the trunk with shade cloth. Pruning is not usually necessary.

Fertilizing: Don't fertilize young citrus for 2 years after installation. I use 20 to 50 pounds of composted dairy cow manure 3 times a year on mature trees, once in February, again in May and September. Aerate around your tree 1 time per month.

Country Garden Companion Planting

The best way to grow gardens is with companion planting. Beans, corn, cucumbers, cabbage and squash grown together make a wonderful garden.

If you're growing tomatoes, plant some basil around them to ward off non-beneficial insects. Basil also wards off flies and mosquitoes. If you like salsa, add some cilantro around your tomatoes.

Other plants that grow great around tomatoes are marigolds, chives (garlic chives are easy to grow), nasturtiums, carrots, lima beans and sage. Always grow marigolds around your garden because they ward off nematodes (parasites in garden soil) and attract beneficial insects. Marigolds and sage discourage tomato horn worms.

Petunias repel aphids.

Always have onions and garlic around your garden. *Note: Avoid using sulfur when planting onions and garlic.* Onions ward off slugs and ants and repel rabbits. Garlic wards off aphids and makes a great detractor for non-beneficial bugs.

If you have a lot of cats hanging around your garden, plant rue to keep them away.

If you have a problem with moths, plant rosemary, artemisia and lavender. These plants grow well in the valley.

Have problems with mice? Plant some mint.

Always grow purple lantana as a trap crop or host plant for white flies. Lantana attracts white flies away from other plants. Kill white flies with soap and water and spray at least every 24 hours.

If you follow these tips, you'll have a beautiful country garden.

Fertilization

Fertilization is the least understood but one of the most important elements of our landscape. Many times, we pour massive doses of fertilizer that is high in nitrogen and then wonder why we have insect and disease problems. These problems are stimulated by high synthetic nitrogen intake that makes our plants more susceptible to insects and disease problems. Plants are not meant to grow in spurts, but through a slow progression of soil building with such products as manure, compost and other natural organic products.

Natural organic fertilizers add humus and carbon to our soil, which is lacking in the Southwest. Along with the benefits of organic fertilization, one of the best is that it is almost impossible to burn the plant if you add a little too much fertilizer.

The following are some of my favorite organic fertilizers:

Alfalfa Meal: It's just plain guinea pig food. I spread it under my roses, vegetables or anything else that needs an extra boost. Citrus trees seem to love it. I also make a tea from it by soaking 1 cup in a 5 gallon bucket and then applying it on my shrub's root system.

Blood Meal: Blood meal mixed with cottonseed makes an excellent lawn food. Spread it with a whirly bird spreader and watch your yard grow without the danger of synthetic chemical fertilizers.

Soft Phosphate: This is used to stimulate flower production. High in phosphorous, it makes sense to work it well into the soil before planting flowers. Try the same technique when planting tomatoes. Plant your plants and seeds right on top of a layer of soft phosphate. 60 percent of newly planted seeds or plants needs of phosphorous are in the first 2 weeks.

Composted Dairy Cow Manure: This is easy and cheap to use to start all vegetable beds. It's great.

Compost: This is the only ingredient you need. You can make foliar tea, fertilize with it and use it for weed and disease control. It can be used on all plants.

Cottonseed Meal: It's high in nitrogen and works great in our high-alkaline soils on lawns.

Fish Emulsion: Emulsion acts as a general insect spray when applied. I use it outside for most of my potted plant fertilization and spray it on my lawn.

Liquid Seaweed: Seaweed can be used as a foliar spray. It will also control spider mites and white flies. Liquid seaweed contains a lot of trace elements and should be the first ingredient used in a foliar spray program because it makes fertilizer and trace elements more available to the plant. Mix it with fish emulsion for an added boost when foliar feeding.

Getting Rid Of What's Bugging You

The warmer weather is going to bring out a lot of insects. One of the best ways to get rid of bugs is to grow healthy plants, so make sure you put a lot of compost on top of the soil (3 to 4 inches thick) and always fertilize organically with blood meal, fish emulsion, or my Extreme Juice. If you still have problems with bugs, try these ideas:

Throw some banana peels around your roses to get rid of aphids.

You can also grow petunias alongside your roses to eliminate aphids.

Artemisia is another plant that every home should have. Make a tea with 1 to 1-1/2 cups artemesia and 1 gallon of water and spray it on your plants. This wards off insects.

Another great plant to grow is pennyroyal. Rub it on your skin for a great insect repellent.

If you have caterpillars, crickets, snails and aphids, gather some up, blend them in a blender and spray on your plants. The live insects don't like to be around their dead comrades.

Tomato leaves also work well as an insect killer. Blend 1 to 1-1/2 cups in a blender, add 1 to 1-1/2 quarts of water, strain then spray on your plants.

Herbal Tea

Good news! Many of the herbs in your garden may provide temporary relief of everyday health problems such as headaches, stress, fever, insomnia and stomachaches. Although medicinal herbs are a valid alternative to traditional medicine, you should see your doctor if your pain persists or becomes severe.

Headache Relief:
Rosemary: Pour boiling water over a sprig of rosemary. Steep for 5 minutes.

Feverfew: At the first sign of a migraine, eat a sandwich made with 1 leaf and 2 pieces of buttered bread. *Note: Do not use if taking anti-coagulants.*

Lavender: Pour boiling water over the flowers. Steep for 5 minutes.

Coriander or Cilantro: Chew the seeds to ease the pain of a migraine.

Sweet Marjoram: Pour boiling water over fresh or dried leaves. Steep for 5 minutes.

Oregano: Pour boiling water over the leaves. Steep for 5 minutes.

Lemon Balm (Melissa Officinalis): Pour boiling water over the leaves. Steep for 5 minutes.

Lemon Grass: Pour boiling water over broken pieces of lemon grass. Steep for 5 minutes.

Stress Reducers:
Chamomile: Pour boiling water over 3 tsp. fresh flower heads. Steep for 5 minutes.

Lemon Balm (Melissa Officinalis): Pour boiling water over the leaves. Steep for 5 minutes.

Insomnia Relief:
Chamomile: Pour boiling water over 3 tsp. of fresh flowers. Steep for 5 minutes.

Lavender: Pour boiling water over the flowers. Steep for 5 minutes.

Stomachache Relief:
Chamomile: Pour boiling water over 3 tsp. fresh flower heads. Steep for 5 minutes.

Basil: Pour boiling water over fresh leaves. Steep for 5 minutes.

Peppermint: Pour boiling water over fresh leaves. Steep for 5 minutes.
Lemon Verbena (Aloysia Triphylla): Pour boiling water over fresh leaves.
   Steep for 5 minutes.

Insects

Lizards, toads, frogs, bats and even insects are great for your garden. Insects do a good job of controlling themselves without spraying pesticides. Did you know only 1 to 2 percent of insects are actually bad bugs?

Chemicals can't tell the difference between beneficial bugs and non-beneficial bugs. So, the best way to get rid of bad bugs is with garden-friendly bugs. The best time to release the friendly bugs is in the spring and one of the best insects to release is the ladybug. Ladybugs are inexpensive, easy to order and ferocious eaters. They'll eat the aphids out of your home and garden.

When you release ladybugs, feed them with a little honey, molasses or yeast. Put it on a little piece of wax paper and hang the wax paper around your garden. That way they won't be going over to your neighbor's for lunch. You may also want to try lightly spraying the ladybugs with a mixture of cream soda. This will keep them "sticking" around. Release them in the evening onto damp foliage.

Also try planting some Alyssum and Cosmos around your house to keep the ladybugs in your garden.

Lacewings are one of my favorites. They are easy to buy, easy to keep and they reproduce often. They'll eat mealy bugs, spider mites, leafhoppers, scale, thrips and white flies.

Trichogramma or moth egg parasites parasitize the eggs of more than 200 loopers, bores, webworms, cutworms and moths.

The praying mantid is a big predator. It will eat everything except lady-bugs. Put the egg cases in the center of a bush; up a little so the ants can't get to them. One egg sack contains about 200 praying mantids.

Mud daubers eat black widow spiders so be careful when you kill the wasps around your home because they're actually beneficial. If they're not bothering you, don't kill them.

Also, make sure you feed your birds all the time and never spray pesticides.

You can order insects through *buenabiosystems.com* and *arbico.com.*

More On Citrus

Citrus is one of the easiest shrubs to grow and a great accent to your land-scape. It is a very easy, evergreen shrub - that's right, I said shrub.

They are meant to be a bush and like a lot of foliage protecting their trunk and fruit. Citrus are not meant to grow like a tree, so be careful where you plant them. They are not meant to be trimmed. The foliage needs to grow as a canopy all the way to the ground.

Citrus grow best in the frost-free areas of the valley and they also need well-drained soil. Before planting citrus, make sure to fill the hole with water and that it drains out completely within 4 to 6 hours.

Depending on the type of citrus you choose, it takes anywhere from 2 to 15 years to produce fruit. Some citrus, such as navels, are alternate bearing, which means they will produce bumper crops every 2 to 3 years. Citrus are also capable of holding their fruit for 3 to 4 months. In fact, you usually will get sweeter fruit the longer you leave it on the tree. Citrus trees have been known to live for 50 to 70 years.

When selecting the variety of citrus tree, make sure you choose a type that is on a rootstock that does well here in the valley, like Sour Orange. It is hard to find a better tree at your local nurseries because nurseries import their trees from California and these types of trees do not have the same qualities that the Sour Orange root stock has.

One more thing, forget about the trees that have a lot of fruit growing on them when you purchase them. Look for trees that have good, low growth with as large of a canopy as you can find. It is also necessary to find a tree that is as small as possible - no larger than 15 gallons - because they are very heavy and if you break the root ball, you will have a tree that will decline in health and eventually die.

When you are planting the tree, you want to dig a hole that is as wide as it is deep. Make sure the hole is no deeper than the root ball of the tree. I personally do not add any amendments to the soil, but top-dress it out to the drip line of the tree with compost.

I also build a large well around the tree beyond the dripline to facilitate flooding the area with water when the tree needs irrigation. I water at 2 to 3 week intervals during the summer once they are established. Over-watering is a major problem, so be careful. I see more over-watering problems with citrus than any other. The best thing to remember is that the moisture must penetrate at least 3 feet into the soil, and make sure the water does not touch the trunk of the tree.

As for fertilizing, I stay completely organic and use 1 to 2 bags of composted manure around established trees in February, May and September. Use this basic guide: Begin with 1/2 of a bag on young (2 years old or younger) citrus for a great start.

There are many types of citrus and taste is the best indicator for what you want to plant. Determine what you want to do with the citrus. Some citrus are better for juicing and some are better for eating. Remember a few varieties will cross-pollinate (like tangerines and tangelos) so plant two different varieties. An excellent resource for citrus selection is *greenfieldcitrus.com*.

Structural Elements

There are many ways to start a garden, but one essential, often overlooked, element is structure. It not only adds dimension to your garden, but structure in any garden provides stable, beautiful areas with which to stabilize your plants. There are three types of structures that work in just about any garden, I've outlined them below:

Teepee Trellis: This structure can be made of wooden stakes, bamboo poles or limbs of a tree (as long as they're fairly straight). This type of framework provides a nice place to grow climbing vegetables.

Concrete Reinforcement Wire Trellis: This structure will soften and cool down the walls around your home and give you a great place to grow melons, grapes, cucumbers, vines, bougainvillea or hardenbergia violacea.

To make this structure: mount one 6-foot by 8-foot sheet of concrete reinforcement wire to two 4-inch by 4-inch by 6-foot redwood posts that have been mounted into concrete. Just let the vines grow up the concrete reinforcement wire and soon you'll have a beautiful trellis.

Wire-wrapped Post Trellis: This simple trellis will help secure climbing roses, pyracantha, bougainvillea and other thorny plants.

To make this structure: wrap a 4-inch by 4-inch redwood post with wire. Secure the post in the ground with concrete. Build a 1-foot by 1-foot platform with a 1-inch lip. Secure the platform to the top of the post. Fill platform with birdseed and you'll have a lovely, thorny bush trellis and a great place for birds.

The Magic Of Mulch

Hot weather is right around the corner! The most critical component to keeping your plants healthy, wealthy and wise will be to mulch the top of your soil. Mulching helps conserve moisture, buffer the soil from temperature extremes and stifle weeds. It also looks nice and increases the tilth of the soil, provides nutrients for the soil, keeps rain from compacting the soil and prevents erosion.

After planting any type of tree, shrub, ground cover, flower garden or vegetable garden, the top of the soil must be covered with mulch. Mulch is not a soil amendment, but a covering placed on top of the finished planting bed after the plants have been installed.

One of the best top dressings is partially decomposed compost. This type of mulch allows oxygen to breathe through the soil surface and enables carbon dioxide to diffuse out of the soil onto the leaves of the plants.

Another excellent mulch is native tree trimmings. This is the mulch I use in my garden at Channel 3. And best of all, I was able to cover the garden with this mulch for FREE! The material can be obtained from many arborists in the area. I like to use cedar or eucalyptus native tree trimmings for their natural insect fighting qualities. In addition, the tree buds, leaves and cambium layer contain protein, which contains nitrogen and other trace elements that are beneficial to our landscape.

I recommend staying away from the pine bark sold at a lot of nurseries. Its flat pieces tend to plate together and seal out oxygen from the soil. But pine needles, when available, make a great natural top dressing.

I also refrain from using plastic material and gravel as top dressings. These inorganic mulches don't biodegrade and don't return nutrients to the soil.

Wildflowers

This spring's glorious wildflower show can be recreated in your own garden - be it a flower-filled meadow, a few pots on a patio or balcony or anything in between.

Wildflower gardening may be enjoyed by all gardeners, from beginners to advanced. Wildflowers can also be incorporated into any style of landscape from naturally wild to a more manicured landscape.

With some planning, some cooperative rain and a little patience, wildflowers will provide beautiful blooming color for you, too.

The fall, especially October, is the best time to plant because the winter rain and cooler temperatures encourage germination of the seeds.

The next best time to plant for summer and fall wildflowers is the month of March. The soil temperatures are still cool and the ground is, hopefully, moist from recent rain. Plant a few packets of seed in your garden. You will be so happy to have those bright splashes of color during those long summer months.

Plant where you can have a reliable source of water. Some years, we don't get enough rain, so supplemental watering is necessary for the seeds to germinate. Some of the seeds may take up to 3 weeks to germinate. They need to be kept moist. But the seeds sure don't want to be blasted with a hose-end nozzle that will dislodge them from their beds or expose them to the birds. Either a watering can or a water wand will work the best to deliver a gentle shower.

Before planting, mix your seeds with potting soil, compost or sand in a ratio of one part seed to four parts filler. This helps distribute the seeds evenly. Sowing your wildflower seeds too thickly causes the seedlings to compete with each other for sun, water and nutrients, resulting in weak and leggy plants.

One method of planting your wildflowers is to sprinkle the seeds directly onto decomposed granite, then use a hose to wash the seeds off the granite and into contact with the soil. If you plant directly in the soil, roughen up only the surface - be careful not to cultivate any deeper than 1 inch. Remember that each square inch of soil contains thousands of weed seeds, most of them waiting for their moment to sprout and grow.

Sow one-half of the seed evenly in one direction, say north to south. Then sow the remainder evenly in an east-west direction. Then go ahead and wash the seed into the granite or press the seed into the soil with the backside of a rake. Don't bury the seeds. They need the sun to germinate. Some of the seeds may not be buried and that's okay.

Another really easy way to start a wildflower garden is to plant a few seeds next to established plants that are on an irrigation emitter. Use the water pattern as a guide and just press the seed into the soil. This way, you'll have wildflowers without having to hand water them. This is a pretty foolproof way to have beautiful flowers. Don't forget to adjust your irrigation clock to water frequently. After the seeds have sprouted and grown a couple of inches, you will need to reset your clock back for your established plants.

A handy tip is to plant a few seeds of each variety in pots of sterile potting soil so that you will know what the seedlings look like when they germinate. This way, you'll be sure to pull the weeds, not the flowers.

Some to try:

- *Desert Marigolds*
- *Gaillardia*
- *Sunflowers*
- *Brittle Bush*
- *Mexican Sunflowers*

Weed often. Weeds compete with your wildflowers for nutrients, water and sunshine.

Thin the wildflower seedlings to give them room to grow and develop their wonderful flowers. It's okay to thin to one plant every few inches.

Another good thing about wildflowers is that you don't need to fertilize them. Once they are up and growing, just water and enjoy them.

If you have chosen plants that are native to the Sonoran desert or are adapted to our climate and soil conditions, they will re-seed in your wildflower garden. Let the seeds ripen for about 2 weeks after the full-bloom period. Then, you can let the plants re-seed naturally or save the seeds in paper bags for later. Or better yet, share the seeds with a neighbor or friend and start wildflowers growing throughout your neighborhood.

When the annual plants have died back, cut them off at ground level. Go ahead and let the roots remain and decompose in the soil to return nutrients to the soil and provide aeration. With perennial plants, cut them back to new growth. Usually, this will spur a new flush of flowers to enjoy all over again.

March Notes:

_____

_____

_____

_____

_____

_____

_____

_____

_____

_____

_____

_____

_____

_____

_____

_____

_____

_____

_____

April 4
Calendar for Organic Gardening

Water
- Water deeply and infrequently.

Prune
- For better light and thicker growth, prune hedges to have wider bottom.
- After bloom, prune spring blooming shrubs and vines. Avoid pruning your cassia and sages into lollipops.

Fertilize
- For newly planted trees and shrubs, apply Extreme Juice monthly in small amounts, to soil as root stimulator.
- Roses and summer flowering shrubs.
- Use Extreme Juice on all plant foliage, adding garlic tea if minor insect or diseases exist.

Pest Control
- For control of thrips on glads, roses, citrus trees and other flowers, release green lacewings or spray with neem.
- To combat ticks, fleas and chiggers use natural diatomaceous earth when weather is dry or apply beneficial nematodes anytime.
- Trichogramma wasps released will help control caterpillars.
- Dust around plants with a combination of cedar flakes, hot pepper and natural diatomaceous earth, spray garlic pepper tea or use beer traps for snails, pill bugs or slugs.

- Blast with water mixed with 2 oz. of molasses per gallon for treating aphid invasions.
- Use beneficial nematodes to control ants. *(arbico.com)*
- Garlic juice plus Extreme Juice is used for treating black spots on roses.

Plant

- Container grown roses, fruit trees and pecan trees.
- Turf grass from seed, sod, plugs or stolens.
- Warm season vegetables: lettuce, large tomatoes, eggplant, beans, cucumbers, squash, corn, black-eyed peas, okra, melons and Chinese long beans.
- Warm season flowers: periwinkles, marigolds, zinnias, lantana, cosmos, portulaca, copperleaf begonias, caladiums, coleus, begonias, nicotiana, 4 o'clocks.
- Flowering perennials summer/fall.
- Summer herbs.

Odds 'n Ends

- Continue turning compost pile.
- Use mulch on all bare soil.
- Use a mulching mower.
- Deadhead roses.

April

Attracting Birds And Butterflies

Here are some tips for attracting birds and butterflies to your garden:

Butterflies: Plant a lot of herbs, including warrow, parsley and sage. Lavender works especially well. If you choose lavender, add a lot of perlite to the soil when you plant it. Also try zinnias. Make sure you use the seeds, not the six packs. Day lilies are also good for attracting butterflies. Check with your local nursery to see which varieties they have.

Here are some other things that work great to attract the beautiful winged creatures: butterfly bush, snap dragons, bee balm and desert milkweed.

Birds: Birdhouses and birdbaths are two obvious choices if you are trying to attract birds. Always keep water in a bird bath. If you choose to hang a birdhouse, make sure you can get into the bottom of it to clean it out. An automatic bird dripper available at Fry's Marketplace, works well to create that running water effect which attracts birds.

Seed-bearing flowers, such as poppies, snap dragons and black-eyed Susan's and cosmos also attract birds. Don't deadhead them, leave seeds on so that the birds will have something to snack on.

Also try berry-producing bushes, such as olive trees and pyracantha (which attract a lot of quail).

If you want hummingbirds to visit your garden, plant red yucca, penstemon, red ferry dusters or cape honeysuckle. Anything with bright tubular flowers attracts hummingbirds, like kids to candy.

Colorful Vines For Fun Or Shade

Vines are a great way to decorate those cinder block walls and blank fences or to complete your outdoor garden room. Here are a few vines for either sunny or afternoon shaded walls.

Vines for Sunny Walls

Bougainvillea comes in many colorful varieties. Be sure to handle the root ball carefully. A broken root ball is a dead bougainvillea.

Campsis Radicans yield lovely orange to red-colored flowers and self-attaches to walls.

Cat's Claw also self-attaches and yields yellow flowers in the spring.

Coral Vine or the queen's wreath grows to about 20 by 20 feet and yields hot pink flowers.

Grapes are fast growing and produce edible fruit.

Lady Banks Rose produces the tombstone rose, the largest in the world, and for this reason needs a sturdy trellis or large area in which to sprawl.

Pink Trumpet Vines yield pink-lavender flowers in the summer.

Snail Vines need afternoon shade and produce lavender flowers that look like curled snail shells.

Vines for Afternoon Shade

Asparagus bean vines bear foot-long beans that taste like asparagus. Plant from seed in April.

Carolina Jasmines bear fragrant yellow flowers starting in January and are poisonous.

Hyacinth Beans are perennials grown as annuals and produce purple or white, sweet pea-shaped flowers.

Pink Jasmine vines bloom fragrant pink and white tubulars in the spring and are evergreen.

Star Jasmines also bloom fragrant white flowers in the spring and the blooms are star-shaped.

Deep Watering

The most important thing you can do for your plants is water them properly. It sounds elementary, right? Well, the way you water is much more critical than how much you water. I have a few tips that will get your plants on the right track.

Water deeply and infrequently. By giving grasses, plants and trees long, wet drinks, you'll have to water less often. To water deeply, turn the hose or drip system on low and let it run for a long time.

The soil has a high pH and holds a lot of salt. When water percolates deeply into the soil, it carries dangerous salts away from the plant's roots. Deeper watering means longer evaporation and will give you more bang for your watering buck.

Move your hose or drip system beyond the drip line or canopy. The ends of a tree or bush's branches mark the drip line - where rain drips during a storm. Well, that's about where a plant's roots reach, too. By watering there, you'll encourage the feeder roots to extend and strengthen the root system. An added bonus is that this will help the plant resist wind damage.

How do you know you're watering deeply enough? Get a soil probe. You can make one with a 5 foot segment of rebar. Simply bend a 1 foot long handle and mark 1 foot increments on the staff of the rebar.

For trees, you should be able to push the staff 3 to 4 feet into the ground; 2 to 3 feet deep for shrubs; 1 foot for ground cover and 6 to 8 inches deep for lawn areas.

Always check your plant and soil to confirm that your watering schedule works for your lawn's needs, and refer to my book ***Extreme Gardening*** for water frequency guidelines. Also, remember to mulch heavily with native tree trimmings to save water and reduce weed growth.

Plants That Cause Sneezes And Sniffles

Allergy symptoms are a sure sign that spring has arrived and most allergies this time of year are attributed to the transfer of pollen or dust-like grains that contain the male reproductive cells of flowering plants.

Plants are pollinated either by birds and insects or by the wind. Wind-pollinated plants cause the most allergy problems. They can be identified by their small, inconspicuous flowers and are typically non-native plants. Because wind pollination is chancy, the plants require an immense amount of pollen.

The kinds of trees pollinated by wind include fruitless mulberries, olives, ash, privets, cottonwoods and mesquite varieties. Shrubs include pampas grass, fountain grass, ragweed, Russian thistle, pigweed, saltbush, rabbit brush and bursage. Ground covers include Bermuda and Johnson grass.

Insect-or bird-pollinated plants also cause sneezing and sniffling, but are identified by their showy, colorful, nectar-producing, fragrant flowers that attract the pollinator to the plant. They do not produce a lot of pollen and have sticky pollen that is transferred from flower to flower by the birds and bees.

Insect-or bird-pollinated plants include Palo Verde, sweet acacia, Ironwoods, lysiloma, desert willow, citrus and palms. The shrubs include cactus, agaves, aloes, yucca, red yucca, Texas rangers, cassias and fairy dusters. Ground covers include lantanas, hybrid bermudas, gazanias, verbenas and primroses. Vines include cat's claw, bougainvillea and coral vine.

You can minimize your allergy problem by planting a varied landscape, avoiding known pollen producers, mowing common Bermuda grass to one inch, spraying olives and mulberries with a flower-prevention product, removing weeds before they flower, staying indoors or under cover in the evening when pollen settles back to the earth and wearing a hat or washing your hair before going to bed to remove pollen.

Summer Gardens

With the hot weather fast approaching, now is the time to plant those heat-loving veggies, prepare the garden and fine-tune the irrigation. Remember that the garden needs 6 hours of sunlight daily, preferably with some afternoon shade. You may want to consider using raised beds because they provide excellent drainage and it's easier to mix in the 2 to 4 inches of recommended compost and mulch.

Artichokes are fantastic, not only for their fruits but also for their strong architectural form and silvered foliage. If you decide to plant artichokes, be sure to plant with a lot of compost, because these guys are heavy feeders. In June, after harvesting the artichokes when they reach softball stage, let the leaves die from heat and protect the plant from our hot sun. Let the leaves remain over the plant to act as mulch and to cool the soil. Reduce watering during this period of dormancy. In August, begin to fertilize with manure or fish emulsion to encourage fall growth.

A beans that needs to be planted soon is the Chinese long bean. This veggie does need support and also needs to be harvested daily during production. Chinese long beans are the only legume that you don't soak before planting as they rot so easily. Also, don't use overhead sprinklers, because you need to keep the leaves dry to prevent spreading diseases. Don't work in the bean patch when it's wet, either.

Nutritious black-eyed peas or cow peas grow really well here and you can harvest them as snap beans or let them mature for shelling.

Corn is also a great hot-weather vegetable and you need to plant early maturing varieties in blocks. This technique ensures good pollination. Corn is a heavy feeder, so don't skip on the compost, rock phosphate and fish emulsion. Remember to fertilize when it reaches knee high. You may also want to mulch thickly with alfalfa hay to conserve moisture. When planting corn, watch out for the corn earworm. Apply a drop of mineral oil to the top of the ear after the silks have turned brown.

Cucumbers are great companion plants for beans and corn because they like the thick mulch around the corn, which will also keep the cucumbers off the ground, preventing pesky critters from munching on their fruit. Be sure to cut the fruit off the vine, instead of pulling on it, or you may break the vine. Planting sunflowers nearby makes for sweeter cukes.

Eggplants also love hot weather, and they produce purple fruit and flowers. Plant several together and harvest the fruit as soon as it's glossy and firm.

Go ahead and plant cantaloupes and muskmelons as well. Enrich the soil with a lot of compost and water deeply. Apply mulch thickly to keep the soil cool and the fruit off the soil and away from bugs.

Okra is a cotton relative that yields gorgeous yellow flowers and can grow as tall as the fence. Pick its fruit daily when 2 to 4 inches long. Cut back by 1/3 in midsummer to encourage a new flush of growth that will continue until frost. Mix cornmeal in soil to prevent fungal diseases.

Summer and winter squash transplants need to be planted now. Again, use a lot of compost, water well and mulch thickly. Harvest summer squash, such as zucchini, patty pan and crookneck as baby vegetables for delicious eating. The flowers are also edible, steamed along with the vegetables. Winter squash needs a long growing season, so plant off to the edges of the garden and wait until the rinds are hard enough to resist the pressure of your fingernail before harvesting.

Another beautiful and delicious summer veggie is Swiss chard, which is a ruby red-stalked plant that will keep producing as long as you keep harvesting the leaves. You can cook the leaves as spinach or slice the mid-ribs and steam or quickly sauté. This plant does better with afternoon shade.

Queen Palms

I get more questions about how to get this ill adapted plant to thrive in the desert. This plant comes from much more humid environments and richer soil then commonly found here in the southwest.

The biggest mistake I see people make is not amending the soil in the area surrounding the tree or the hole the tree will be planted in.

When planting these trees, be sure to add at least 1/2 compost to 1/2 of the indigenous soil. Also, mix in 1 pound of Volcanite, and 4 to 5 pounds of Texas Greensand. Texas Greensand contains manganese, which is essential for the survival of queen palms.

Once you have mixed these ingredients together, place the tree on a bed of rock phosphate in the hole and back fill with the soil mix.

You must water the plant and keep it on the moist side. I also top-dress the soil surrounding the palm with 4 to 6 inches of compost and top-dress that with native tree trimmings.

Queen palms also like to be planted in groups, or among other trees to prevent wind damage and like the feet densely planted with shrubs such as asparagus ferns; this keeps the soil cooler and acts as a living mulch.

Once they are established, I fertilize often (every 2 to 3 weeks) with light applications of bat guano, Rocket Fuel, or Extreme Juice along with top dressing the soil surrounding the palm with Texas Greensand occasionally; especially older queen palms.

Queen palms like their feet a little on the damp side with occasional deep watering, at least 1 time a month and remember you have to fertilize often. Also, remember to mulch with 2 to 4 inches of compost with a top dressing of native tree trimming.

Tropical Fruits

Allspice is the easiest of all tropical spices to grow and will grow to heights of 4 to 8 feet. They yield fragrant flowers and berries, which are used as spices. Evergreen allspice is hardy in the cold down to temperatures in the mid-twenties.

Avocados are also good bets, but you must choose grafted varieties and those named for the low desert. Grafted varieties may produce fruit as quickly as 2 years from planting, but seedlings may not produce for 10 years and flavor quality varies extremely. When planting, keep in mind that 2 varieties are needed for pollination. Avocados grow large, but need humidity during flowering for fruit set. Misters work best to supply the necessary moisture. Also, planting avocados in groves supply shade and more humidity. Avocado trees also need filtered sun, good drainage and a well-composted soil mix. They grow best with east or southeast exposure or against a south-facing wall.

Guavas are the easiest to grow of all subtropical fruits if you choose the right variety. Varieties include the *Bangkok Apple Guava #2*, which tastes best when still green and crunch. *Tropic White* and *Tropic Pink* varieties taste best when they show yellow. Strawberry and lemon guava varieties need to be planted in full shade and watered frequently, up to four irrigations a week. Guava trees grow to 12 feet tall.

Other tropical fruits that grow well in the low desert include dwarf bananas, which produce fruit in 2 to 3 years and don't need to be watered in the winter. Mexican papayas love the sun and heat, do not need water in the winter, but do need protection from the cold. *Kent* or *Nan Doc Mai* mangos need to be planted near a southeast wall for protection. Also, do not use fertilizer the first 2 years and do not over-water. Key limes also grow well, but need protection from cold and frost and grow best in containers. Pineapples need protection from frost.

These plants may be purchased at Tropica Nursery, 3015 E. Baseline Road, Phoenix. For information, call them at (602) 576-6948 or visit my web site.

May 5
Calendar for Organic Gardening

Water
- Deeply and infrequently.

Prune
- After their blooming, deadhead your roses.
- Spring flowering vines, shrubs and trees after they bloom.

Fertilize
- Citrus.
- Lawns.
- Use an organic fertilizer on all potted plants and annual flowers.
- Every 2 weeks spray all foliage with Extreme Juice.

Pest Control
- Weed using mechanical devices or organic weed killers.
- Release lacewings and ladybug.
- Use food grade diatomaceous earth in dry weather for fleas, and ticks. Beneficial nematodes are good anytime especially on damp soil.
- For pecan case bearer and caterpillars release trichogramma wasps.
- Bacillus thruingiensis helps with cabbage loopers, other caterpillars and grape leaf skeletonizers.
- For aphids on tender, new growth use a powerful water spray.

- Wash spidermites off of evergreens.
- Apply cornmeal (10 to 20 lbs. per 1000 sq. ft.) for brown patch or fungal diseases in soil.
- Spray garlic-pepper tea or citrus pulp for ants.

Plant

- Trees and shrubs.
- Mandevilla, penta, hibiscus, bougainvillea and others for tropical color in beds or pots.
- Time to plant hot weather vegetables and ground covers from pots.

Odds 'n Ends

- Leave clippings on lawn as you mow weekly; stay with organic fertilizers. Use electric mulching mowers.
- Add new matter and turn compost pile.
- Add mulch to all bare soil.
- Collect wildflower seeds

May

Bug Battle

You're probably used to getting rid of bugs with spray chemicals. But, with so many insects this summer, you're only going to get the first wave, then another group will hit. You don't want to keep spray chemicals around your home because many are lethal and most are illegal except for use by pesticide companies.

You may hear malathion is not bad because it breaks down. That is not true. It becomes even more dangerous as it breaks down. Diazanon contaminates the ground-water and kills bird life. It is so bad, it's illegal on golf courses. Please don't buy it; it's very dangerous.

So, in this chemical war, you lose.

Here is a battle plan to avoid problems and still get rid of bugs:

Artillery: Mix a solution of 1 to 2 tbsp. diatomaceous earth per gallon of water and put in a sprayer. It's great for getting rid of crawling insects, such as ants, cockroaches, ticks and fleas.

Grenade: Put a cup of diatomaceous earth in a new sock and tie the open end. Shake it to distribute the diatomaceous earth evenly.

Land Mines: Mix 1 cup sugar and 4 tbsp. boric acid. This is great for killing roaches. You can also mix a solution of equal parts sugar and clothes detergent.

Smart Bombs: There are some insects you want around your home, such as ladybugs, lacewings and praying mantis. So, to kill just the bad bugs and not hurt the beneficials try BioNeem. It kills fungus, aphids and whiteflies. Read the back of the bottle for mixture amounts. Use in a sprayer.

Barbed Wire: Certain scents ward off insects. Plant society garlic, basil, geraniums and santolina around your house.

Chemical Warfare: Make garlic-pepper tea. Simmer 1 clove garlic per quart of water. Let cool; grind and mix in jalapeno peppers. Use in a sprayer.

> *For grasshoppers:* order Nosema Locustae from *arbico.com*.
> *To kill mosquitoes:* use BTI. Order this at *arbico.com*.
> *For ants:* try diatomaceous earth, pyrethrum or boric acid. You can also try simmering ground lemons, letting them cool, then using as a spray. Never use boric acid outside around your plants.
> *To find scorpions:* you need to hunt them with a black light. Seal all cracks to eliminate them.
> *Don't kill spiders:* because they eat insects.
> *Be sure you alternate the products you use.* Don't always use diatomaceous earth or BioNeem. Use different tactics so bugs don't build resistance.

Distracting Animals

This is the time of year you can get overrun with birds, rabbits, deer and other critters looking for a free handout or thinking your garden is the local restaurant.

If you're like me, you love animals and hate the thought of hurting them just to be able to grow a garden. In my travels, I have found some natural solutions that help. Remember one thing - a lot of companies will come out and trap the critters for you, but once you release them into another part of the countryside, their chances of survival are slim to none. This is especially true for snakes, which, by the way, are excellent rodent controllers.

Speaking of snakes, one of the best ways to discourage them from taking up residence is to control your rodent population. I plant catnip, onions and spearmint in and around my house and garden to discourage them from hanging around. You might also try moth balls and camphor oil to discourage them. If you still have snakes, you might want to try Dr. T's Snake-A-Way. They are located in Pelham, Georgia or visit *www.pestproducts.com.*

If you live in the desert, rabbits seem to be a never-ending problem. I sprinkle the ground around my garden with human hair, blood meal, bone meal and Epsom salts. If all else fails, I use 3 feet of one-inch mesh chicken wire with at least 6 inches buried under the ground. You can also wrap young trees with the same type of wire if they are chewing on the lower trunks of your trees.

Right now birds are my biggest nemesis. They wait until my fruit is nice and perfectly ripe, then they help themselves until they have ruined everything. I find that hanging fake fruit in my trees works. I also do this with my tomatoes and grapes. You might also try bird netting, covering up your fruit trees and tying small paper bags around the grapes. If you have birds roosting on your window sills, ridges or ledges around your home (even tops of signs) try Tanglefoot. Bird Tanglefoot is a non-drying, long lasting sticky material that does not trap birds but gives them a sticky ledge that makes them uncomfortable.

Last but not least, dogs and cats are warded off by mustard oil. You can get this at Lee Lee Oriental Market in Chandler. You might also grow a plant called rue. Dogs and cats round out the circle by doing an excellent job of getting rid of rats and mice, which make it less likely that you will have snakes.

Eradicate The Bad Guys

Summertime seems to be the worst and best time to find insects in your soil, depending on what type of bugs you find. But, fear not, there are some earth-friendly ways to eradicate those bad guys.

First, start with clean soil. In the desert climate of the southwest, we are able to do what some of our neighbors cannot do: take advantage of our heat and solarize our soil. This is a simple process of tilling in a little compost, wetting down the soil and then covering it with clear plastic. Leave the plastic on top of the soil for 4 to 6 weeks and voilá! You have a nice, clean, pest- and weed-free garden ready for fall planting. *Hint: If you have vincas and tomatoes in the garden prior to solarizing, I add ground-up broccoli to my soil to get rid of a disease called verticillium wilt.*

When getting ready to purchase seeds, always look for the letters V (stands for virus), F (stands for fusarium wilt), N (stands for nematodes), and T (the tobacco mosic virus) after the name of the seed. These seeds have been bred to resist diseases. Always remember to prune out dead wood seedlings. Plants like to be thinned out and don't like to hang out with their sick buddies.

Remember to water plants deeply and infrequently and always early in the morning. I like to use a drip system that allows me to soak the root system pushing all the salts deeply into the soil. Always pull weeds completely out of the ground before they have a chance to take over. Weeds not only compete for water but also nutrients, sunlight and restricted airflow throughout your garden.

Remember to deadhead your flowers for a continuous bloom and remove all decaying fruit vegetative matter, etc. This will help keep down any fungus, insects and diseases that have a tendency to invade our gardens in the summer.

I use insect traps this time of year to control white flies and other small critters that like to munch or suck on my plants. You can order them from Arbico. I use beneficial insects to get rid of aphids, ants, white flies, fleas and ticks. *Remember: Don't use any chemicals at all, they kill the good bugs as well as the bad.*

Rotate the type of annuals, fruits, vegetables and other crops you grow year to year. By planting the same type of plant in the same location, you are building up specific pests and diseases that will wait to attack the plant the next time you plant. Rotating crops also keeps vital nutrients from being depleted.

Lawns

You need to start thinking about getting your lawn in shape for summer, so here are a few tips:

Increase your watering time to allow for 1 to 3 inches of water per week and only water in the mornings. Also, check your sprinklers to make sure they are functioning correctly.

Aerate your lawn. This allows oxygen to penetrate into the soil to create a healthy environment for the roots. Also, rake some compost and soil sulfur over the yard after doing this. De-thatch lawns in the summer if needed.

Treat your yard to a good feeding. I like to go organic, so try some steer manure or cottonseed meal, or foliar feed with Extreme Juice.

If you really want to help your lawn, try spreading about 20 pounds of sugar per 1,000 square feet over the lawn to help the microorganisms in the soil.

Only cut 1/3 of the leaf stem when you mow.

Lighting For Your Landscape

You can buy a standard lighting kit at most home centers and they are easy to install, but here are a few hints:

Try to buy metal fixtures. They hold up better than plastic.

Point the light so you can't see the source of the light.

Lighting fixtures are not meant to be seen.

Try direct lighting of light-colored foliage and tree trunks. Light-colored objects show up much better than dark-colored objects.

Fit the fixture to the situation. Buying a kit may not fit your situation.

Use a flashlight to try to simulate a lighting scheme in your yard.

Don't bury your wires until you are sure of your location. Try several locations to find the perfect spot.

Don't create a runway effect along your sidewalks and driveway.

It's the lamp that does the lighting not the fixture, so spending a lot of money on lights is not necessary to get a great lighting effect.

Mother's Day Flowers

Are you thinking about purchasing flowers for your mom this Mother's Day? Well, there are a couple of things to keep in mind for better-looking, longer-lasting bouquets.

When you're buying cut flowers, freshness is the key. I know you might want to get your mom roses, but think twice before plunking down the cash. Roses are one of the only flowers that can be kept in a chemical dry storage for up to 6 months, and it's not uncommon for that to happen.

Listed below, you will find freshness indicators, flower care and alternatives to the classic bouquet of roses.

How do you know if a flower is fresh?

Color: Look for vibrant, consistently colored leaves and petals.

Firmness: Stay away from flowers with wilted petals.

Bruising: Carefully check the stems for signs of bruising.

Discoloration: Brown leaves and stems indicates a lack of freshness.

Other than roses, what flowers are long lasting and pretty enough for Mom?
Mums
Carnations
Alstroemeria
Miniature Carnations

How should flowers be cared for?
Use sterilized pruners (sterilize with solution of 10% bleach to 90% water) to trim at least 1 inch off each flower's stem. Should you need to, further trim your flowers under a stream of lukewarm water. Fill a sterilized vase with lukewarm water and add your own preservation solution *(see recipe below)* or a prepackaged solution like Flora Life. Make certain to change the vase's water once each day.

How can I make my own flower preservation solution?
Add 1 tablespoon of sugar, 2 tablespoons of lemon juice (fresh only) and 2 teaspoons of bleach to a quart of water. Depending upon the size of your vase, place 1/2 cup to 1 cup of this solution in a vase of lukewarm water. An alternative to this solution is to add 1/2 teaspoon of bleach to a can of 7-Up or Sprite; place 1/2 to 1 cup of the solution to a vase of lukewarm water.

Remember: If you purchase fresh flowers, have your mom trim the stems and change the water every day, and she'll have a beautiful Mother's Day remembrance from her loving children.

Pets And Pests

When your dog or cat comes into the house, it could bring some unwanted guests with it. Ticks and fleas are a major problem this time of year, but you don't have to resort to a stinky flea bath or collar. There are some natural remedies and simple chores you can do to get rid of them.

Oranges and eucalyptus leaves can get rid of fleas and ticks. Give your pet a citrus bath. Boil orange peels in water for several minutes. Let cool and rub onto your dog. Use eucalyptus leaves and cedar bark as filler for a dog bed.

Diatomaceous earth can get rid of fleas and ticks, too. You must remember to use food grade diatomaceous earth, not the kind for your pool. Sprinkle it on your pet's food. It's so "pet friendly" you can even dust your pet with this fine powder. A light dusting around your yard will ward off unwanted pests, as well. You can also add brewer's yeast, bee pollen or garlic powder.

Pet waste is a breeding ground for pests, so clean it up often.

Rake and sweep a dog run often.

Vacuum your home frequently. If you find fleas and ticks, try sprinkling carpets with boric acid, diatomaceous earth and baking soda. Leave for 3 hours then vacuum. Check behind hanging pictures for outbreaks of baby ticks.

A good product to try in your yard is Pyretheum. Mix 1 tablespoon with a gallon of water and spray around your yard. Also, try adding a tablespoon of vinegar to the dog's water dish. This helps to ward off insects.

Mix potato starch and water and put the paste around the base of trees. Ticks will climb into it and get stuck.

Planting rosemary, sage, eucalyptus, artemisia, and santolina are great ways to ward off bugs because their scents keep pests away.

To remove a tick, pour hydrogen peroxide on it.

Scorpions

If you've never seen a scorpion up close, our rising temperatures might cause that to change. The summer's heat brings the scorpion population to life. As long as you're aware of them, though, you shouldn't be afraid. Here are a few tips to help make you aware of the types of scorpions in the desert, prevent infestation and more:

Types of Scorpions:

Giant Hairy: 2 to 4 inches long, dark brown, hairy, cannot climb vertical surfaces

Bark: less than 2 inches long, tan or brown color, smaller and more poisonous than other scorpion varieties, can climb vertical surfaces

Where Scorpions Live:

Scorpions like to live in humid areas of your home. For instance, foundations, woodpiles, ground covering, wet paint or other liquids are especially appealing to scorpions. Take extra caution when working near such areas.

Ways to Prevent Scorpion Infestation:

Consider ground covering with plants that grow several inches off the ground.

Seal all cracks and seams near your baseboards, around pipes at sinks and faucets and in block walls.

Pick up woodpiles and debris from your yard.

Spread food-grade diatomaceous earth and pyretheum along areas where you want to ward off insects.

Put Tanglefoot (found at Fry's Marketplaces) at the seam of your door-stops. The sticky material prevents scor-pions from passing over.

Use plants to encourage snakes, toads and lizards to live in your yard.

Use a safe, organic product to kill individual scorpions and cut down on the number of breeding scorpions in your area. I recommend using Orange Guard or Bioganic Pest Control. You'll have to spray the product right on the scorpions in order to kill them, but these products certainly do the job. For more product information, visit *www.GardenGuy.com.* SealEze sells a sweep to put on the bottom of your doors to ensure protection from pests. This is available at s*ealeze.com.*

For Parents of Infants: I recommend protecting your sleeping child by putting a glass jar under each leg of your child's crib, as bark scorpions are unable to climb glass.

Summer Lawn Hints - Of Course, The Natural Way

It's summer time and taking care of your lawn becomes an important part of your lawn's life. I have found that the organic way is the only way to fully enjoy that lawn. You won't have to worry about those dangerous pesticides, herbicides or synthetic fertilizers. By going organic, you are encouraging the beneficial macro- and micro-organisms that do so much to maintain the natural balance. To get your lawn in tip-top shape, you'll have to take care of a few things, like controlling weeds, fertilizing and watering.

Aeration: You'll have to aerate your lawn because compaction of the soil has likely reached such a degree that it will require additional oxygen to survive the warm summer months well. After aeration, you should top-dress your lawn with a 3/8 inch layer of compost, which contains many disease-fighting organisms. By aerating and top-dressing this time of year, you'll be taking care of your lawn's fertilizing needs as well.

Note: *If you don't own an aerator, you can rent one at most equipment rental locations.*

Watering: This is a critical element in creating and maintaining a great lawn. It will take anywhere from 1 to 3 inches of water per week, depending on a combination of three elements: wind, heat, and the amount of shade your lawn receives. As a general rule, I water my lawn every other day, and I water it only in the morning.

Note: *You'll need to use a screwdriver or probe to make certain that the water has penetrated at least 6 to 8 inches into the soil.*

Mowing: Depending on how hot it is, I mow off no more than 1/3 of the leaf blade, which might require mowing as often as every 3 or 4 days during the monsoon season. Make sure your blades are sharp and try to use one of the new mulching lawn mowers; this will reduce your fertilizing needs by at least 1/3.

Fertilizing: See the aerating and top dressing instructions above; do this at least twice each year. Always use organic fertilizers. Try to stay as organic as possible.

More On Summer Lawns

Who doesn't like the look of a nice, green lawn? It creates a feeling of coolness around your home, plus the dark green adds such a wonderful texture and richness. To get all the benefits of a beautiful lawn, though, now is the time to get to work.

A few basic grass rules:

1. *Lawns need to be planted away from your home.* When planted too close, watering the grass can cause the soil to expand and contract and damage the foundation or pool decking. Also, putting grass too close to the foundation of your home can break the termite barrier created when the home was built or treated.

2. *Lawns need well-drained soil.* Otherwise, sitting water will attract mosquitoes, which can lead to encephalitis or heartworm problems in pets.

3. *Lawns need well-prepared soil.* Working compost into the soil will go a long way toward avoiding excessive water and fertilizer and it helps to fight disease problems.

4. *When you water, make sure the moisture penetrates 6 to 8 inches deep each time you water.* Use a long screwdriver or a soil probe to determine the water is getting deep enough.

5. *Fertilize only with organic material:* compost, blood meal, liquid seaweed, Extreme Juice, etc.

The type of lawn you choose and its maintenance needs all depend on how much sun or shade the grass will get during the day. If you've got trees or walls that leave your grass in shade for most of the day, think about using Dichondra or Saint Augustine.

For lawns that get full sun, I am a big proponent of the new hybridized types of Bermuda, such as Santa Ana, Midiron or Bobs-od (Bull's-Eye Bermuda). If you would like to try some great seed varieties, use Majestic or Blu-muda. Both take full sun well & can be mowed with rotary-style or mulching mowers.

If you would like to check out other varieties of grasses, go to *www.westernsod.com*.

Over the last 5 years, my opinion of lawns has shifted. I now believe that lawns need to be as small and easy to care for as possible. They use a tremendous amount of water and fertilizer (as well as synthetic pesticides, herbicides and fertilizer), not to mention the gasoline for your mower and your time to mow them! All of this has a tremendous environmental consequence, especially if synthetic chemicals are being used, which can leach into our water supply.

The bottom line is to keep your lawn as small as possible, use only organic materials and keep your lawn healthy to prevent disease or pest problems.

The natural way is the best way to enjoy a summer lawn.

The Best Ways To Water

It's hot and time to adjust your water cycles up for your trees, plants and lawn.

The basis of watering is to water deeply and infrequently. Deep watering is making sure the water penetrates the full depth of the root system. On trees, this is normally 1 to 3 feet, 1 to 2 inches on shrubs and 6 to 12 inches on lawns. If the water does not penetrate as deep as the root system, you will find your plants to be shallow-rooted, always stressed for water and they will sometimes show stress from lack of nutrients. Every time I water, I use a 3 inch long rebar stake that I push into the soil to check the depth the water has penetrated. Then I adjust the length of time I water up or down to suit the plant's needs.

Make sure you water on the outside drip line of the tree (the drip line is the edge of the tree or plant canopy). These are the roots that absorb the moisture necessary for your plants' survival.

Spreading granite, mulch, compost or bark helps retain water in the soil.

This not only reduces watering frequency, but helps increase the amount of beneficial micro flora and microorganisms that are necessary to the plants or trees overall health. For irrigation frequency, remember, *"deeply and infrequently."*

This Way Is Mulch, Mulch Better

What would you say if I told you about one little thing you can do for your plants that will reduce watering needs, increase the disease-fighting capabilities of the plants, help them become more heat tolerant, and add to the overall health of the soil? You'd probably say, "Wow, Garden Guy, I always knew you were brilliant!" It's mulch.

I wish I could take credit, but the idea really belongs to Mother Nature. So what's so great about mulch? Several things.

Mulch conserves soil moisture, increases water percolation and moderates soil temperatures. It acts like a layer of insulation and if you use organic material (which I suggest), then it will also help invigorate the soil as it decomposes. Along with all of this, mulch decreases competition from weeds and increases micro biotic activity at root systems. All of this helps our plants resist disease while cooling down the soil and helping to build a plant's heat resistance.

Anytime you plant a tree, shrub or flowerbed, spread a 2 to 4 inch thick layer of mulch on top of the soil. Unless it's compost, don't mix the mulch in. Simply allow it to rest on top of the soil, but don't let it sit against the trunk or stem of your plant. Mulch should be at least 2 inches away from the trunk or stem of the plant and out past the drip line of a tree. This will help protect both the budding roots of the plant and the soil. In fact, you should always cover bare soil with some type of organic mulch.

If you're wondering which type of mulch to buy, here are a few of my favorites:

Alfalfa Hay: This is my first choice of mulch for areas planted with vegetables (especially this time of year). It retains moisture and releases a small amount of stimulants that enhance growth.

Bark: I recommend using larger bark chips because smaller chips tend to smash together and create a seal that prevents oxygen from reaching the soil. And as you know, oxygen exchange is crucial to healthy plant growth.

Compost: Compost is one of the best top dressings you can use. It makes all types of plants and trees healthier. However, one of the downfalls to using compost is that it tends to blow away in strong winds. *Hint: Add a top layer of large bark chips or stones to hold it down.*

Eucalyptus or Cedar Bark Chips: Both act as natural insecticides and are great for dog runs.

Alternatively, you can make mulch from items commonly found in your yard. Simply follow my tips below.

Grass Clippings: Blend with leaves and apply a 2 to 4 inch thick layer.

Leaves: Spread the layer so that it is no more than 4 to 6 inches thick. Consider composting the leaves first.

Pine Needles: Spread a 5 to 8 inch thick layer. Pine needles are slow to break down and have a low pH.

Shredded Tree Trimmings: Apply a 4 to 6 inch deep layer. Arborists might even give you this for free!

May Notes:

June 6

Calendar for Organic Gardening

Water
- Outdoor potted plants twice a day.
- Deeply and infrequently.

Prune
- Shrubs and trees need dead and damaged wood removed.
- Blackberries' new growth to a 3 foot height to enhance side branching after harvesting.

Fertilize
- Use organic fertilizer on all planting areas.
- Apply Texas Greensand to help with iron deficiency, which results in yellowed leaves.
- All plantings and lawns should be sprayed with Extreme Juice every 2 to 4 weeks.

Pest Control
- Dust with natural diatomaceous earth or release beneficial nematodes for fleas, ticks and chiggers.
- Spider mites can be controlled with Extreme Juice sprayed every 3 days for a total of 9 days.
- Release trichogramma wasps for bagworms and other caterpillars. A spray with Bacillus thuringiensis will work also.
- Garlic-pepper tea or summer weight horticultural oil will remove lace bugs and elm leaf beetles.

- Use Extreme Juice plus garlic tea for black spots on roses.

Plant

- Pumpkins for October harvest.
- Palms and cacti.
- Start fall tomatoes from seed.
- Desert trees, shrubs, palms and cacti.
- Bermuda and St. Augustine lawns.
- Periwinkle, lantana, cosmos, verbena, portulaca, amaranthus.
- Tropical colors of hibiscus, pentas, mandevillas, bougainvillea.

Odds 'n Ends

- Leave clippings on lawn as you mow weekly.
- Add new matter and turn compost pile.
- Add mulch to all bare soil.
- De-thatch your summer lawn if needed.
- Start harvesting grapes.

June

Caring For Your Lawn Without Chemicals

With the banning of Durasban from homeowner use, it won't be too much longer before most synthetic fertilizers, insecticides and herbicides are carefully monitored and possibly banned from use.

There are many ways to fertilize and control weeds and pests without using chemicals. Here are a couple of ideas to help you create a safe environment around your home.

During times of heat and drought, try mowing higher. This helps to discourage weeds and reduces water stress. Mowing higher in shaded areas help to keep it greener.

Mow only 1/3 of the leaf surface every time you mow. This will some-times mean mowing every 3 to 4 days during the summer.

Use only organic fertilizers. Also, use blood meal, cottonseed meal or just top-dress your lawn 2 to 3 times a year with compost or steer manure. By going with organics versus synthetics, you may not have the most beautiful lawn, but you will be able to leave your grass clippings (without contributing to our landfills) on the ground to decompose. You'll also rest assured that your kids can play in absolute safety, not worrying that you may have poisoned your yard with dangerous chemicals.

Leave your grass clippings on the yard now that you're using organic fertilizers and mowing less than 1/3 of the leaf surface every time you mow. Your grass clippings will decompose and contribute 1 to 2 pounds of nitrogen per 1,000 sq. ft. per year. This will take care of approximately 1/2 of your fertilizer needs every year.

Always mow your lawn when it is dry. A wet lawn will make your blades dull.

Always use a sharp blade.

Water early in the morning and make sure the water penetrates at least 4 to 6 inches every time you water.

Don't use herbicides on your lawn. Not only are they dangerous, but also they are not needed to create great lawns. If you have a weed problem, it always leads back to how you care for your lawn. It will help to mow your lawn a little higher so the grass chokes out the sunlight weeds need to grow.

Don't use insecticides on your lawn. I find that insecticidal soap, diatomaceous earth, Neem and beneficial nematodes are great for getting rid of 90 percent of the insect problems. For the other 10 percent, I use mechanical means or live with it. Never use dangerous pesticides.

Aerate your lawn regularly. Oxygen is added through aeration, a process of top-dressing with compost and gypsum and punching holes into your lawn on a regular basis. Twice per year is perfect. You can either buy an aerator or rent a machine for this purpose.

Last but not least, spray your lawn down once per month with liquid seaweed. Not only does it have trace elements in it to help with your lawn's fertilizer needs, but it contains elements that help build disease resistance and reduces heat and drought stress. Try 15 oz. per 1,000 sq. ft. of lawn space. For an extra boost of nitrogen, try mixing a little fish emulsion.

You may not have the perfect lawn, but you will have a lawn that you can rest assured has no poisons that may contaminate the environment or hurt your kids or pets. Along with all of this, you will also find more birds, lizards, earth-busting earthworms and insect-eating toads to help make your garden a place to call home. *Remember one thing: The healthier your lawn, the fewer pests, disease and chemical fertilizers you will need to keep it looking great.*

Compost

As you probably know by now, I whole-heartedly believe in the benefits of composting. The natural breakdown of organic material makes for an incredibly useful product around your home. It increases the fertility and tilth of the soil, suppresses weeds, retains moisture and increases micro biotic activity that is so crucial to our soil.

Did you know that nearly 20 percent of materials in a landfill can be composted? One-fifth of everything we throw away could be re-used, including kitchen scraps (no meat, though), tree trimmings leaves and more. If you think that it's important to recycle, then this is a chance for you to help Mother Nature do some recycling of her own.

Compost is one of the best sources for enriching soil fertility, suppressing weeds, retaining moisture and increasing the beneficial micro-fauna and micro-flora in the soil. I predict that in the next 10 years, composting will be required of all homeowners in the valley.

Composting is done with both solid waste, such as kitchen scraps and newspapers, and sewage disposal. At my cabin I use a composting toilet, and I have experienced no problems. Composting is one of the best ways to give back to the environment without adding to our landfills or polluting our water supply.

An easy way to start a home composting operation is to first build a container. This can be as simple as a trench, 2 by 3 by 4 inches, or a trash can with approximately 20 to 40 - 1/2 inch holes punched into it. My favorite way is to take 8 alfalfa hay bales and stack them into a square. The city of Phoenix will also sell you a compost bin for $5 to $10. Their number is (602) 534-3333.

The next step is to fill these containers with the proper ingredients. Half of the ingredients must be browns and may include sawdust, straw, twigs, newspaper and dry leaves. The other half of the ingredients must be green and may include old vegetables, fruit peels, landscape trimmings and grass clippings. The fresher the better.

Blend the green material and then blend the brown material. Layer the brown and greens into your bin, adding a little blood meal as you go. I sprinkle about 1/4 cup per cubic foot of compost. Blood meal acts as a boosting agent.

The biggest problem is that the bins have a tendency to get a little dry. I solve this by installing a drip emitter system on top of my pile to keep it about as moist as a wrung-out sponge.

Last, but not least, the pile must be turned once a week or you can try a little trick I have used, which is adding sunflower stalks to the pile as you build each layer. The stalks are hollow and do a good job of getting oxygen into your compost pile, eliminating the need to turn the compost pile.

If I were limited to only one thing to garden with, it would be compost. It has all the magical qualities necessary to create outstanding desert gardens.

Irrigation Tune-up

Here's a handy irrigation checklist:

Clean out all of your sprinkler heads.

Check the screen and spray nozzles for any debris that may have built up during the winter months.

Clean your drip heads by soaking them in 1 part vinegar to 10 parts water for 1 to 2 hours. This will remove any hard water deposits that have built up inside the heads.

Reset your timer for watering early in the morning. As we get into higher humidity, your plants and grass need to dry out during the day.

Make sure your drip heads or bubblers are watering at the edge of the drip line of the tree. Use the drip line of the maximum diameter of the tree. The roots of your trees absorb moisture at this point. They do not absorb moisture at the trunk.

And last but not least, use your soil probe and follow the water schedule in my book, ***Extreme Gardening***.

Organic Controls

There is no reason you should spend a lot of money on fertilizers, weed killers and insect control products at the store. Most of the time they are made with dangerous, synthetic chemicals that we shouldn't put in the house or ground, anyway.

Below are a few recipes for organic controls that use ingredients you probably already have in your cupboards:

Solarizing the Soil

Supplies: *Shovel*
              Clear plastic, enough to cover the desired area
              Rocks

Instructions: Till the soil, then water deeply. Cover the area with clear plastic; place rocks atop plastic to hold it in place. Leave plastic covering on for 2 to 4 weeks.

Note: *This method is best for getting rid of weeds and diseases in new and existing gardens.*

Gin Weed Control
Supplies: *1 oz. gin*
1 oz. apple cider vinegar
1 tbsp. baby shampoo
1 quart water
Pump spray bottle

Instructions: Mix ingredients together; pour into a spray bottle. On hot summer days, spray mixture on foliage. Repeat as necessary.

Alcohol Weed Control
Supplies: *1 quart water*
1 to 5 tbsp. of rubbing alcohol
Pump spray bottle

Instructions: Mix ingredients together; pour into a spray bottle. On hot summer days, spray mixture on foliage. Repeat as necessary.

Outdoor Ant Control
Supplies: *1 to 2 gallons water*
Stove or barbecue grill

Instructions: Heat water to 160 to 170 degrees. Quietly sneak up to the mounds of ants and pour the boiling water down the hole.

Note: *I normally try to do this between 11 am and 2 pm.*

Indoor Ant Control
Supplies: *1 tbsp. boric acid*
1 tbsp. mint jelly or peanut butter
1 cracker
Small cardboard box

Instructions: Mix the boric acid and mint jelly; spread mixture on a cracker. Punch pinholes in a cardboard box; place cracker inside. Place box in an area where ants cause problems, but away from children and pets.

Note: *The mint jelly or peanut butter lures the ants in and the boric acid kills them.*

Indoor and Outdoor Ant Control
Supplies: *Diatomaceous earth*

Instructions: Dust food-grade diatomaceous earth along the ants' pathways.

Note: *The white powder will cut through their exoskeleton and they will dehydrate and die.*

Indoor and Outdoor Ant Control
Supplies: *1/2 cup Cream of Wheat*

Instructions: Place a dish of Cream of Wheat where the ants can access it.

Note: *After they eat it, the cereal expands and the ants will explode.*

Cockroach Bait
Supplies: *1/2 cup sugar*
1/2 cup boric acid

Instructions: Place sugar and boric acid in a mason jar lid. Place lid in areas away from pets and children.

Note: *The roach is attracted to the sugar and the boric acid kills him.*

Ornamental Shrub and Plant Fertilizer #1
Supplies: *1 tbsp. Epsom salt*
1 gallon water

Instructions: Combine ingredients, then spread on the soil.

Ornamental Shrub and Plant Fertilizer #2
Supplies: *1/2 cup apple cider vinegar*
1 gallon water

Instructions: Combine ingredients. Pour mixture around ornamental plants in your yard.

Note: *Everything gains advantages from the low pH and trace elements. This mixture also helps fight whiteflies and thrip problems.*

Coffee Ground Pick-Me-Up
Supplies: *1 cup coffee grounds*
2 cups water

Instructions: Spread coffee grounds on a newspaper to dry. Apply dried coffee grounds to the ground around your plants. Alternatively, mix coffee grounds with water and spread on desired area.

Patios

With the hot weather here, it's a great time to put in patios.

One of my favorites is called Holland stone. This brick is especially easy to put down because it is already pre-fitted. No cutting is required and it fits together easily. Level your area and put down a pre-emergent followed by a weed barrier fabric. Set the brick to the size you want. After you finish putting the brick down, sweep sand between the cracks and you'll have yourself a beautiful ready-made patio. You can install 100 square feet per hour.

Another great way to put down a patio is to use cobblestones, which are available at home centers. These are fake stones that look real and are great for garden pathways. Plant thyme or dichondra between the stones for a European look.

One of my favorite ways to get an instant patio is to use stabilized granite. This is granite that has the glue built right in it. Spread the granite out on top of your soil and roll it with a heavy sod roller or a tamper. It turns almost as hard as concrete. It is a great natural look for pathways or patios. It's very easy to put in a curve-linear design. Call Stabilizer Solutions in Phoenix at (602) 225-5900 for details on this popular product.

If you are thinking of putting in a wooden deck, use Weyerhaeuser products, which make a line of plastic wood. You can screw the pieces together or cut them like real wood. They'll look just like a real wooden patio. These are sold at home centers.

Plants To Plant

Landscaping during the summer can be filled with all kinds of danger. I would advise that you drink a lot of water and wear a big hat. However, there are certain types of plants that should be planted this time of year.

One of these is the saguaro cactus. They can be purchased bare root. They should be planted in unimproved soil and should never be watered, except when Mother Nature provides it. Some other types of cacti you might try are the ocotillo, hedgehog and barrel cactus. The barrel cactus is one of my favorites because it has a funny way of always growing to the south.

Other indispensable plants that I always use in my landscape are Mexican fan palms, California fan palms and California date palms. They all grow well in the southwest and can make a great over-story for garden areas. They should be planted in areas that get afternoon shade. Once installed, they need a lot of water to get established. Once established, you will find they are easy to grow with occasional water and fertilizer.

If you currently have Mexican fan palms, California fan palms or California date palms, go ahead and trim the flower spathes (seed heads) and some of the foliage. Everyone has a tendency to trim their palms back too far, so be careful and get sound advice before trimming.

Desert-type plants are something else you may want to plant this time of year. Try sage, cassia, desert fairy dusters, Palo Verde, ironwood and mesquite. All these transplant well during the summer monsoon.

Summer Watering Schedule

Lawn: Water 2 to 3 inches per week at 1/2- to 1-inch intervals. Watering should only be done in the morning. Try the footprint test: If you can see your footprint, your lawn needs more water. Moisture must penetrate at least 2 feet into the soil.

Small Plants and Shrubs: Water them until you can press a probe down 1 to 2 feet into the soil. Water every 5 to 10 days.

Trees: Water them until you can press a probe down 2 to 3 feet into the soil. Water every 10 to 20 days.

Mulch: Place 2 to 3 inches around trees and shrubs. Keep the mulch 2 to 3 inches from the trunks and stems. This will help in conserving water. Mulch out to the drip line of the trees and shrubs.

Water Stress: The best time to look for signs of stress in your trees and shrubs is early in the morning, not late in the evening.

Drip System: If you have a drip system, make sure the drip emitters are dripping at the drip line, not against the trunks and stems.

To keep the micro biotic activity in your soil active, give an extra dash of fish emulsion and vinegar once a week to all potted plants.

Summertime Tips

Summer is here and I have a few tips to help you make your plants a little less stressed out because you didn't take them to the mountains or beaches.

Paint citrus trees and other fruit trees, like apricots, apples, peaches, etc., with 50% latex paint and 50% water. It acts like sun block and keeps your plant trunks from sunburning.

Prune your palms.

Keep an eye out for powdery mildew. It looks like a white film on your leaves. Spray the leaves with 1/4 cup of baking soda and a drop of dishwashing soap per gallon of water.

Do you have a monster eating your plants? It may be a leaf cutter bee building her home for the brood. Don't worry, be happy. She won't do any damage. You can tell if a leaf cutter is doing the damage if there are perfectly round bites taken out of your leaves. She doesn't hurt the foliage at all.

Start to remove old cardboard boxes and debris from around your house to avoid an infestation of roaches. You might want to treat the area along your walls with diatomaceous earth to kill any roaches possibly lurking out there.

Give your citrus a good fertilizing with 1/2 bag of steer manure for a 2 to 6 year old tree and a full bag for a mature tree. Remember, your tree begins its birth the day you plant it and should not be fertilized the first 1 to 2 years.

Tea For Tulips (And Other Plants)

It's teatime in my garden! I've got some natural and organic brews that are easy to whip up and are absolutely fantastic at increasing a plant's micro biotic activity, lowering the pH, increasing trace elements, increasing humus available to plants (a powerful nutrient) and bolstering their immune systems.

Manure Tea: Put about 10 handfuls of manure in a woman's stocking. Place the stocking into a bucket with 2 to 5 gallons of water. Allow the mixture to stand for 4 days in the summer, 10 days in the winter. Remove the stocking and use the tea to drench soil around plants.

Benefit: Stimulates macro and micronutrients in the soil.

Alfalfa Tea: Fill a 2 to 5 gallon bucket with water. Place as much alfalfa hay as possible into the bucket, making certain there is enough water in the bucket to soak the hay. Let the mixture stand for 4 days in the summer, 10 days in the winter.

Don't strain the mixture before pouring it around your plants. If your plants have plenty of mulch, then strain the mixture before soaking the ground with it.

Benefit: Provides growth enhancers and regulators.

Note: *In December, put this tea in a sprayer and help your Christmas tree stay fresh and live longer. It's also useful for preserving cut flowers.*

Oak Leaf Tea: Use oak leaves to fill a 5 gallon bucket, 1/3 to 1/2 full. Pour boiling water over the leaves, then strain the mixture and drench the soil around ornamental plants. Use the leaves as a mulch to add potassium to the soil.

Benefit: Helps increase root strength.

Note: *For an added boost, include oak leaves in any other plant tea.*

Compost Tea: Place 10 handfuls of compost in a woman's stocking. Soak compost in 2 to 5 gallons of water. Let the mixture stand for 4 days in the summer, 10 days in the winter. Strain mixture into a spray bottle and use as a foliar spray to help fertilize your plants.

Benefit: Stimulates micro biotic activity.

Note: *For added plant protection, try adding one or more of these helpful items after the tea has brewed:*

Apple Cider Vinegar: Add 2 tablespoons per gallon of tea for added trace elements and substantially lowered soil pH. Apple cider vinegar also helps plant roots more effectively gather nutrients. Use a spray bottle to apply the mixture to the foliage.

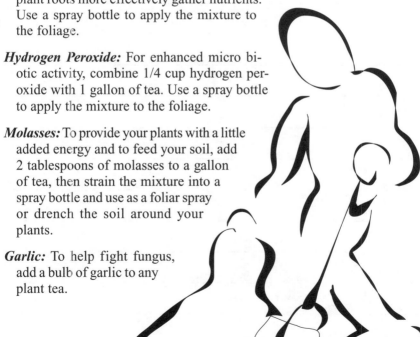

Hydrogen Peroxide: For enhanced micro biotic activity, combine 1/4 cup hydrogen peroxide with 1 gallon of tea. Use a spray bottle to apply the mixture to the foliage.

Molasses: To provide your plants with a little added energy and to feed your soil, add 2 tablespoons of molasses to a gallon of tea, then strain the mixture into a spray bottle and use as a foliar spray or drench the soil around your plants.

Garlic: To help fight fungus, add a bulb of garlic to any plant tea.

June Notes:

July

Calendar for Organic Gardening

Water
- Deeply and infrequently.
- Daily watering for outdoor container plants.

Prune
- Limbs that are dead or damaged.
- Remove old flower heads from flowering plants to encourage new flower production.
- For fall blooms, trim roses.

Fertilize
- Texas Greensand is used for iron deficiency.
- Use organic fertilizer for all planting areas if not done previously in June.
- Use Extreme Juice to spray on all foliage.

Pest Control
- Remove cochineal scale from prickly pear with strong blast of water.
- Drench fire ant mounds with citrus pulp.
- Dusting with natural diatomaceous earth and applying beneficial nematodes helps rid fleas, ticks, and chiggers. Soil sulfur works great, too!
- Spray spider mites with garlic-pepper tea or spray with liquid seaweed.

- Dust chinch bugs with natural diatomaceous earth.
- Use hands or a hula hoe for removing weeds.

Plant

- Desert trees and plants.
- Warm seasonal lawn grasses.
- Start seasonal vegetables for a fall garden like tomatoes, peppers, melons from seed indoors.

Odds 'n Ends

- Leave clippings on lawn after mowing.
- Add new ingredients and turn compost pile. Start new piles, adding molasses to eliminate any fire ant problems.
- Bare soil should be mulched with partially completed compost or other coarse textured material.
- Reduce heat stress on plants with regular applications of liquid seaweed.
- Move potted plants to areas that receive early morning sun and afternoon shade.
- De-thatch Bermuda lawns.

July

Cactus Care And Cooking

Some folks I work with at 3TV have asked me recently about problems they are having with cactus. And I'll tell you what I told them: *Most problems with cactus stem from too much water.* Most people tend to over water, but it's also possible that the soil is not draining well enough and the roots of the cactus are just sitting in water.

You have to remember that cacti are desert plants. They are used to arid, dry conditions and, in fact, they favor them.

If there is too much water, a rot can form. For transplanting cactus, add a little powdered volcanite and soil sulfur to the soil as you plant. It will help the roots establish.

So to solve 99 percent of cactus ailments, reduce your watering and make sure the soil is well-drained.

And while I'm talking about desert plants, I'd like to mention the edible kind. There are a lot of desert plants you can use in your cooking, or you can use to survive if you're stuck in the desert.

Bon appetit.

Purslane: Purslane can be eaten fresh, cooked in stews or soups, boiled or steamed. It can even be dried for future use. The following is a recipe for a great salad:

1 cup purslane stems or leaves
1/2 sliced onion
1 cup diced tomato
1/2 cup cilantro

Combine together and enjoy!

Tumbleweed: Young raw tumbleweed tips can be chopped and eaten with salads. They can also be steamed, boiled or sautéed. They are great in omelets. Here is a great recipe for creamed tumbleweed:

6 biscuits
1 cup tumbleweed, chopped
1 tbsp. butter
2 tbsp. flour
1 cup milk
Pinch of basil
Salt and pepper to taste

First steam the tumbleweed for 5 to 10 minutes. Then melt the butter in a pan and slowly stir in the flour. Gradually add milk and lower the heat. Continue to stir until thickened. Season the sauce with basil, salt and pepper. Drain the tumbleweed and add to the sauce. Serve over sliced biscuits.

Prickly Pear: You can eat the pads and the fruit of the prickly pear. The fruit (known as tunas) can be eaten raw or made into a juice by peeling the outer skin of 24 tunas (its easier to peel them if you boil them first). Then strain the seeds and mix 1 cup of sugar and a quart of water. Chill and enjoy!

The pads (known as nopales) can be used in many wonderful recipes. The following are just a few of many:

Nopales Salsa: Over a newspaper, carefully remove the thorns by scraping the pads with a knife. Cube the pads and bring to a gentle boil. Strain the pads and then put in fresh water bringing back to a gentle boil. While boiling add cubed pads. Boil for 15 minutes. Strain and serve with corn chips.

Mesquite: Boil pods or eat raw.

Yucca: You can eat the flower petals raw or boil fruit for 10 minutes. Slice and serve with butter.

Hot Weather Tips

Use chelated iron or Texas Greensand on your lawn for a quick green-up without the mowing. It's a great way to go, especially if you foliar feed. This basically means to spray it on your lawn.

Plant pumpkins in the next 2 weeks for an October harvest. Pinch back the vines and reduce each vine to one pumpkin to create that giant Charlie Brown pumpkin.

Hold off on pruning sun- or salt-damaged foliage until September or October. The damaged or dead foliage protects the plant from further damage.

Remember the best time to plant palms and grass is right now. Try out the new hybrid Bermuda grass seed on the market. I have heard of some fantastic results. These new varieties seem to stay green longer during drought and take less fertilizing and mowing. Look for the blue certification tag when purchasing these new seeds.

If you have potted plants, protect them from the sun by inserting your existing pot into a larger pot and then insulate the space with peat moss, sphagnum moss or newspaper. Also remember to apply a slow-released fertilizer, such as compost or fish emulsion, every time you water.

Making Pots

Pots are a big part of how we garden and landscape our homes. They are great at helping control things like water, fertilizer and soil content. The fact that they're easy to move around also means we can control how much light a plant receives and its air temperatures.

But to do a little potted gardening, you don't have to go out and spend a lot of money. Why not try making a few self-fertilizing pots yourself? Your plants will thank you for it.

Pot 1

Ingredients: *1 part Portland cement*
1 part vermiculite
1 part peat moss

Note: This mix was fairly easy to work with, held its shape well and has a light, spongy feel.

Pot 2

Ingredients: *1 part QuickCrete*
1 part peat moss
1 part perlite

Note: Because QuickCrete contains large pebbles, this mixture is a little more difficult to work with. It does, however, produce a nice, earthy-looking pot. But if you prefer a smoother-looking pot, substitute QuickCrete mortar mix for the recommended QuickCrete.

Instructions for Pots 1 and 2:

Combine ingredients. Mix in just enough water (about 1 gallon) to create a "mud pie" consistency.

Line a large pot with plastic; tape plastic down on outside edges. Place a 2 inch layer of the concrete mixture in the bottom of the pot; level the concrete mixture out by hand. Place a smaller plastic pot inside to create a pot form. Evenly fill area between the large pot and the small pot with the concrete mixture. Pack the mixture into place and put it in the sun to cure.

Note: Sprinkle the pot form with water every few hours to keep the new pot from cracking. Your new pot should be ready to use in about 24 hours.

Recommended materials are available at most home improvement stores.

Natural Insect Repellents

With the hot, rainy weather, expect to see a lot of insect activity, but don't go purchase a bunch of pesticides. Pesticides kill a lot more good insects than bad ones. Pesticides also kill lizards and toads and can make you and your pets sick.

One of the insects you're going to see in the next couple of weeks are mosquitoes. Try draining standing water or treat your water with B.T.I. You can purchase this at Arbico, 1-800-827-2847, or Peaceful Valley, 1-888-784-1722. You can also try a thin application of vegetable or mineral oil sprayed on the surface of the water. Do you have a birdbath? Just add some citrus peels to the water.

I have already noticed some white flies flying around my pumpkins (plant them right now for an October harvest) and lantanas. These small white flies can do a lot of damage if you don't try to control their numbers. Try putting some aluminum foil underneath the plant to reflect sun onto the bottom sides of the leaves. I also spray them down with soapy water (about 1 tbsp. per gallon of water) or just drown them with a spray of water. It works great.

If you have ants, try feeding them Cream of Wheat. Apply it dry and when they eat it, the cream of wheat expands in their bodies and kills them.

Plants that are natural insect repellents are lemon grass, santolina, penny royal, peppermint, artemisia, tansy and eucalyptus. Growing these around your house eliminates your pest problems.

No-Till Vegetable And Flower Gardens

With September fast approaching, you need to start putting together a garden and I've got a fast, easy solution for you.

First, find a place that has full sun most of the day, 4 to 6 hours are best, and afternoon shade is okay. Apply a thin layer of soft phosphate and blood meal to the bare soil.

Next, take some newspaper and lay it on top of the ground about 1/4 to 1/2 inch thick. I like to soak it in water first and lay it down because it does not blow away and starts getting the microbes excited about future possibilities.

Now, put down about 6 to 8 inches of manure.

Lay another layer of newspaper on top of the manure. Again, lay it on after soaking it in water.

Then, lay about 8 to 10 inches of straw on top of the newspaper. After this, lay black plastic over the top and let it cook in our summer heat for 4 to 6 weeks.

You can plant directly into the straw with six-packs of vegetables or flowers. While you're planting your six-packs, install soil around the plant. Make sure you build your gardens no more than 3 to 4 feet wide for ease of access.

Outdoor Summer Pots

The incredible heat of our summers makes potted plants suffer. You can ease that suffering, though, by doing just a few simple things.

Always use light-colored pots.

Always use insulated pots. Styrofoam pots are the best, but can be costly. If necessary, insulate your existing pots by nesting them in other pots and fill the space between the two with packing peanuts, newspaper or straw.

Never use a pot that holds fewer than 5 gallons in size. Anything less allows the soil to heat up too quickly and cook the roots.

Pots and soil must drain well. This is imperative. Make sure that each time you water, you can see the water running out the bottom. This flushes away deadly salts and also assures you're giving the roots a good drink.

Don't let pots sit in a pool of water. Stagnant water encourages disease, rot, mosquitoes and more.

If your soil needs drainage assistance, add Perlite to your soil.

Add mulch to the top of your soil. Use pine needles, oak leaves, alfalfa hay or straw as a layer of insulation over the soil around potted plants. This will help retain moisture, maintain a constant soil temperature and fertilize the soil.

Fertilize often. About once a week, hit your plants with a natural fertilizer like fish emulsion, liquid seaweed, apple cider vinegar or Extreme Juice.

Water regularly.

Use proper potting soil. I recommend a mixture of equal parts vermiculite, perlite, peat moss, compost and manure.

Polycultural Gardens

Have you ever driven down the road and noticed row after row of crops flashing in the field next to you? If so, you've experienced monoculture. That means only one plant (or one dominant type of plant) is grown year after year in the same place, draining the soil of nutrients.

Most farms, whether they grow corn, lettuce or cotton, are monocultures. They often depend on massive amounts of insecticides, herbicides and chemical fertilizers to stimulate unhealthy soil. Eventually, monocultures produce food with fewer nutrients and more chemical content and they create a measurable negative impact on our environment.

At the other end of the spectrum are polycultures - the environments that encourage plants, insects and animals to strengthen one another. And I think it's the way to go for home gardens and lawns. A polyculture in your landscape will provide organic-style vegetables, fruits, flowers, nuts and herbs. They will be more nutritious, taste better and will contribute to a healthier environment. Plus, organic gardening is cheaper.

At my home, I have not used a synthetic chemical in 10 years. And in the last several years, my home and garden have gotten into such balance, that I have not needed controls, organic or otherwise, for my garden. Bugs take care of themselves. Disease doesn't have a place to grow, and birds and wildlife are there to lend a helping hand.

If you're just starting a garden, build up the soil with plants like beans and peas, then get some shade going with a canopy of trees (preferably in the legume family) on the west side of the yard. Once that's done, add pathways, raised gardens and sheet mulch to create a wonderful polyculture made up of a variety of flora and fauna.

Along with good produce, beautiful scents and glorious views, a well-designed yard and garden have other benefits, including promoting good health. With a balanced polyculture haven for plant life and beneficial wildlife, you can stop using deadly chemicals around the house. Besides the bugs, who breathes and absorbs those harmful substances? Every living creature, including your kids and pets, that's who.

We still don't know all of the long-term consequences of chemical use, but substituting natural techniques for synthetic ones will help you and everyone else in the long run.

Trees That Provide Shade

When planting trees, there are a few things you need to consider. One is how much shade do you really need? If you have a lawn or garden nearby, it is imperative that both get at least 4 to 6 hours of morning sun.

Another consideration should be litter. How much litter your tree produces will usually determine how much work you will have to do in the future. Leaf litter isn't all bad. I use mine for compost, bedding for animals and as ground cover that retains moisture in the soil. Obviously, you do not want trees that litter fruit and leaves near a driveway, entryway or pool. Some low-litter trees to consider are the ficus, fruitless olives, palm and southern live oaks.

Last, but not least, you should consider the fertilizer and water requirements of the tree. Believe it or not, some of the least water- and fertilizer-intensive trees are not ones you would consider. When compared to a southern live oak, the mesquite tree looks like a sumo wrestler who was taken off his diet. It is critical that you consider the watering and fertilizing needs of a tree before you make a purchase. Some low-care trees include oaks, evergreen elms, Palo Verdes, ironwoods, acacias and ficus.

Palo Verdes, ironwoods and acacias all belong to the legume family and do not need fertilizer to survive. In fact, synthetic fertilizer has been known to shorten the lives of some trees and may also stunt their growth. A few other fertilizer-light trees you might consider are ash, cottonwood (in flood-irrigated lots, far from your home septic tank and pool), and Texas ebony (has thorns and will ward off any intruder hiding in a dark corner).

Remember, when purchasing a tree, smaller is better. The larger the tree, the longer it takes to come out of transplant shock. A small tree will usually outgrow a larger tree 2-to-1. I like to start my trees from a 5 or 15 gallon bucket. The largest I like to plant is a 24 inch box tree. Also, always check to make sure the tree's roots are not root bound and have a nice, green, uniform appearance.

Good luck and cool planting.

Water Gardens

Adding a water garden to your home's outdoor environment has some fantastic benefits. Not only are they beautiful to see and hear, but they attract insect eaters like hummingbirds and dragonflies.

In a well-balanced water garden, the fish clean the water by eating algae and their waste fertilizes the plants to stimulate growth. Such ponds are relatively inexpensive and easy to set up.

To build your own, gather the following materials:

1/2 whiskey (or stoneware) barrel, 12 to 16 inches deep (the deeper, the better)

1 pond liner, pre-formed if possible

1 water pump, should pump 140 to 200 gallons per hour

20 bricks

1 plug with a ground fault interrupter (GFI)

1 extension cord

1 bog plant (i.e., water clover, umbrella palms, tropical water cannas, water pennywort, iris and water lilies)

Several handfuls of floating plants (i.e., shellflower, water hyacinth, duckweed, azolla and salvinia). *Note: Floating plants bob on the surface of the water and don't need soil. If they reproduce quickly, simply thin them from time to time.*

2 - 1 quart underwater grasses (i.e., anacharis or vallisneria)

Fish: 2 goldfish or 12 mosquito fish

Setting Up Your Pond:

Place your whiskey barrel in an area that gets morning sun and afternoon shade.

Use a hose to drench the barrel with water until it swells, then place the liner inside. *Note: If the liner sits too low, put enough play sand in the barrel to raise the liner.*

Place several bricks in the bottom of the liner, then set the pump on the bricks before you add the water. If the pump is the right height, you'll see bubbles at the surface of the water.

If desired, add a pond primer like Pond Perfect (for more information, call The Lily Pond at (602) 273-1805).

Wait a few days before adding plants to your pond - the water needs to detoxify and algae needs to build up.

Adding Plants To Your Pond:

Place bricks inside the pond to create multilevel surfaces for the plants.

Submerge plants to oxygenate the water. *Note: Roots need to be submerged in soil, however fertilizing is never necessary.*

Wait 2 to 3 weeks before adding goldfish to your pond or 3 days before adding mosquito fish.

Adding Fish To Your Pond:

Float fish on the top of the pond for several minutes in the bag they came in. This will allow the fish to acclimate to the pond's water temperature.

General Pond Maintenance:

About once each season, you'll notice the crown of the plant has grown above the soil line. This indicates that it's time to re-pot your plants. To do so, simply place a little sand on the top of the dirt to keep soil from coming out.

Change your pond's water once or twice each week (about 16 oz. each time). If it's available, fresh rainwater is excellent to use when you refill your pond - its pH is perfect. Only blooming plants need fertilizer.

August

Calendar for Organic Gardening

Water
- Deeply and infrequently.

Prune
- Palm trees.
- To stimulate regrowth and more blooms.
- Trim spent flower stalks and blossoms from annuals.
- Trees and shrubs need dead and damaged wood removed.

Fertilize
- Citrus, flowers and vegetables.
- Roses.
- Use Extreme Juice every 2 weeks to foliar feed all planting beds and lawns.

Pest Control
- If needed release beneficial insects: ladybugs, green lacewings, praying mantids.
- Grub worms are controlled with good soil culture. If needed, apply beneficial nematodes.
- Dust natural diatomaceous earth for chinch bugs.
- Use Extreme Juice and garlic tea for aphids. Water blast and release ladybugs. For better results add 2 oz. of molasses per gallon of spray.
- For individual mounds of ants use soapy water or diatomaceous earth. Broadcasting orange or grapefruit peeling pulp aids also.

- For borers in peach, plum or other fruit trees use organic fertilizers, and dust diatomaceous earth around the bases of trees. You can also inject beneficial nematodes into the holes.
- For chewing insects use a dusting of natural diatomaceous earth, spray with Extreme Juice or broadcast beneficial nematodes. For insects that are harder to control, use 2 oz. orange oil per gallon.

Plant

- Tomatoes
- Divide iris and transplant.
- Plant wildflower seed.
- This is the last month to install newly seeded Bermuda lawns.
- Warm season lawn grass planting should be finished. Fertilize Burmuda with Texas Greensand.
- Your fall colors should be planted - mums, asters, marigolds, zinnias, & celosia.
- Also fall flowering bulbs - fall crocus, fall amaryllis, spider lilies.
- Get ready to plant fall and cool season vegetables - lettuce, carrots, beets, radishes, English peas, cauliflower, broccoli, brussel sprouts, beans, corn, melons, squash, cucumber.

Odds 'n Ends

- Leave grass clippings on lawn as you mow weekly.
- Turn the compost pile.

August

Easy Ways To Irrigate

My work takes me all over the valley and I'm finding that every place I go, summer has taken its toll on plants and people alike. The ongoing dry, hot and windy conditions have done a fair amount of damage to my roses, citrus and other ornamentals. To keep plants as healthy as possible in this rough weather, you have to keep deep watering them. Covering them with cheese cloth or an old white sheet is also a good idea.

Back to the deep watering. Irrigation is essential, but it doesn't have to cost a mint. There are several cost-effective ways to create and maintain drip systems that will keep your plants watered and healthy.

One way to irrigate involves either a 1 gallon milk jug or a 5 gallon paint bucket. Make sure they're clean before using them - you don't want to contaminate the water. Drill a small hole in the bottom of your jug or bucket. It should be no larger than 1/8 inch. Fill the container with water and place it near the drip line of a tree or shrub. The water will slowly leak through the hole into the ground without running off into adjacent soil.

In this heat, you're probably already running your air conditioner. Why not put it to another use? I connected a hose to my air conditioner condenser drain line and ran it out to different parts of my yard to deep water my shrubs or trees. This type of water is very low in salts and does not contain toxins such as chlorine. That means it's great for watering potted plants both indoors and outdoors. I would like to offer a word of warning, though. Never let the water accumulate right next to your house. It will attract termites and other nasties.

My last suggestion is a system known as water harvesting. This one depends on Mother Nature. I've installed plastic trash cans under the areas of my roof that collect the most water when it rains. I use the rainwater on my potted plants. I either use a bucket to carry the collected rainwater across the yard or, with some plants, I simply dip them in the container. One other way to use this water is to install a small submersible pump and connect it to a hose or small drip system.

Edible Wild Greens

One of my favorite things to do is to identify wild edibles. It's the kind of hobby that harks back to the days of Daniel Boone or Davy Crockett. I am sure they did not eat fresh bear meat every day they lived out in the woods. I bet they ate a lot more wild vegetation than they ate meat.

Well, back to the subject at hand. Edible plants are quite prevalent here in the southwest and some are quite tasty. One of my favorites comes from the cactus family and is called the prickly pear.

It is the easiest plant to find in the desert and both the fruit and pads are edible. The fruit is easy to identify with its deep purple color. When it is ripe, you can eat the inside and it tastes like a fig.

You can normally find them in the fall. Be careful, the fruit and the young pads have small thorns, some almost microscopic, that will get into your hands. I use a rolled-up full-length piece of newspaper and wrap it around the fruit and twist it off.

Mesquite trees are one of the most prolific types of vegetation you can find in the desert. Not only is its wood great for smoke flavoring when cooking (I soak it in water overnight and then put a couple of pieces on my barbecue grill when cooking), the pods are also great for making a cold tea. Take 20 to 30 pods and let them set in 1/2 to 1 gallon of water overnight, strain the liquid and enjoy. The pods are about half sugar and have a slight vanilla taste.

Next time you want a fresh salad, add some tumbleweed to it for an extra burst of flavor. Now don't go out and pick any old tumbleweed; use the young ones. They have a tangy taste. I have had the older plants and used the tender tips steamed or boiled. I know of a chef in town that actually sautées them in a crab dish. When cooked, they have a mild-flavored taste that will mix with any other type of greens.

One of my favorite types of wild greens to grow is called purslane. It has a creeping habit with succulent leaves and tiny, bright yellow flowers. I let it grow around my rose garden as a companion plant, but I also mix it in my salads. It goes great with a little onion, cilantro, tomato and a little oil and vinegar dressing. As with most greens, try to pick the youngest growth for the best flavor.

With all wild things, use discretion and moderation when eating and picking. Remember, leave some for the wildlife to enjoy.

Food For Foliage

When I talk about fertilizing, I usually tell you to feed the soil, then let the soil feed the plant. It's a great way to help plants get strong and grow healthy, but foliar feeding is an even faster organic way to get food to the plant.

Almost every plant on earth is able to absorb moisture and nutrients from the surface of its leaves. When foliar feeding, it's even more important than usual to use natural organic fertilizers. This useful technique is not only 300 to 400 times more effective, it can actually ward off insects.

To apply foliar fertilizers correctly, spray it on both sides of the leaves. I recommend using a pump spray bottle or a hose-end sprayer. Make sure to apply the fertilizer lightly on young leaves. You don't want to spray so hard that it rips the leaves off of the plant.

I recommend spraying the foliar feed on damp, humid mornings. This will give the plant time to absorb the food and it also allows the leaves to dry out and avoid potential disease.

Houseplants

One way to keep up with your plant-growing hobby during these hot days is to grow indoor plants. Most houseplants are easy to grow and you might want to try some of the varieties for low- and high-light areas.

Some great plants for low-light areas are the bird nest fern, lemon-lime dricantha and neantha betta palm. Plants for high-light areas include the peace lily, pink polka dot and the rubber tree.

To care for your houseplants, make sure they do not sit in trays that are flooded with water because they do not like their "feet" to be wet. Occasionally, I spray the leaves of my plants with some hydrogen peroxide to help the beneficial microbes. Each time I water my plants, about once a month, I add 1 to 2 tsp. of vinegar and 1 to 2 tsp. of fish emulsion. I also place my plants in the shower to wash the foliage of any nasty bugs that might be living there and to wash out any salts that may have accumulated in the pot. One more hint, your air conditioner dries out the air and most houseplants are tropical. Try grouping them close together and place a bowl of water in the middle to increase the humidity a little.

Houseplants For Healthy Air

With the heat and air pollution alerts seemingly being common items these days, a lot of us are spending more and more time indoors. Well, I have bad news and good news.

Number one is that sick-building syndrome and air pollution cause sneezing, burning eyes and cancer and has been linked to Sudden Infant Death Syndrome (SIDS).

The good news for all of this is that houseplants can help you fight off all the effects of chemical contaminants that have a tendency to build up, with time, in our home or office.

Some houseplants are better than others in removing contaminants from your indoor environment. NASA has done some major research on what are the most effective plants to remove certain types of chemicals that cause sick-building syndrome.

One of the most prolific chemicals that permeates our indoor environment is formaldehyde. It is used in the manufacturing of fabrics, carpets and other consumer products. Some of the plants that you might want to try, especially if you have a newer home or office, to help remove formaldehyde are:

Chrysanthemum or Mums, which need a lot of morning light and need to be kept lightly damp to moist and well drained.

Janet Craig also works and is a great low-light indoor plant, which needs damp soil. It also needs to be fed fish emulsion every 2 weeks and the leaves need to be wiped down.

Rubber Plants work well and need morning sun and dry soil. They grow best when fertilized every 2 weeks. Allow soil to dry between watering.

Some of the best all-around plants to remove xylene, toluene, ammonia and alcohol-based indoor pollutants are indoor palms. I have some of these palms inside my office to not only create a relaxed atmosphere, but to remove the contaminants. Some of the best palms include:

Areca Palms, which grow well in semi-sun and damp soil. They need to be fed every 2 weeks.

Lady Palms fare well when misted regularly and grown in semi-shade. They need to be kept damp to wet and fed every 2 weeks to a month.

Bamboo Palms are great for increasing the humidity inside your home during dry summer months. Add a lot of water to keep them damp and fertilize every 2 to 4 weeks.

Some plants that are easy to grow and remove indoor air pollution that any brown thumb can grow are:

Golden Pathos, which need to have their leaves kept clean with a damp cloth. Let soil dry between watering.

Mother-In-Law Tongue is the easiest to take care of and is a plant that will last a lifetime. They like to be on the dry side and will tolerate complete shade and thrive on lack of care.

These are just a few of the plants that will help you stay mentally as well as physically healthy and at the same time, you get the enjoyment of creating your own tropical environment inside your home.

Hydro Gardening

Your own fruits, vegetables and flowers can be grown, with better results, without the excess labor of traditional gardening methods. Today's gardener is aware of high-efficiency growing techniques like hydroponic gardening or "hydro gardening" and has learned the benefit of high-intensity discharge light and safe pest controls in the garden. You can produce more productive plants in less time with much less work.

Hydroponic techniques have been used for centuries. The earliest known hydro gardens are the Hanging Gardens of Babylon, the Floating Gardens of Kashmir and the Aztec people of Mexico used rafts on shallow lakes to grow plants. More recently, mobile hydro gardens were used to feed soldiers during World War II in the South Pacific.

Put simply, hydroponics is the science of growing plants without soil. The same natural elements that are necessary for plant growth in soils are used with the advantage that weeds or soil-borne pests do not restrict your plants.

Instead of growing in dirt, where nutrients and water are randomly placed, the plant is fed a nutrient-rich watering solution. This allows the plant to grow faster, resulting in a larger harvest of vegetables, fruits, herbs and flowers.

Hydro gardening is a highly efficient method of growing plants. In a hydro garden, the nutrients and water are delivered directly to the plants' roots, allowing the plants to grow faster and harvest sooner simply because the plants are putting more energy into growing above the ground instead of under it.

Hydro gardening also allows for higher yields than soil, as you can grow more plants per square area. This is because the plants do not have to compete with weeds or each other for food and water.

Another advantage of hydro gardening is the versatility of location and not being subjected to weather and climatic factors. A hydro gardener has the choice of growing outdoors or indoors with the use of high-intensity grow lights. Indoor grow lights replicate the sun's spectrum. The gardener is then able to control the day length for the plants.

Hydro gardening has been used commercially since the 1970's. Much of the produce purchased in grocery stores is greenhouse- or "hothouse"-grown, using hydroponic methods. The consumer demand for environmentally friendly and quality products has been a major factor in creating the popularity of hydroponic gardens for the individual. Using hydroponics, the gardener knows exactly what has gone into the plant and can make sure that no harmful pesticides have been used.

A hydro garden can be as simple as a plant in a pot filled with rock or some other type of growing medium that is watered by hand. The water must contain the elements required for plant growth that the plant doesn't get from the air. Water mixed with these elements is called the nutrient solution. Watering a hydro garden by hand may be impractical with more than a couple of plants or with a grow substrate like grow rock that will dry out in a few hours. Most hydroponic gardeners utilize a hydro garden that is automated with pumps and timers to do the work for you.

Get your hydro garden and supplies at Sea of Green in Tempe, (480) 967-2045, *www.sea-of-green.com.*

Make Your Home More Secure With Landscaping

Security should always be a factor when landscaping your home. Think about directing pedestrian traffic to well-lit areas with low-voltage lighting. Make sure it is bright enough with the use of a halogen bulb. Incandescent bulbs do not create enough light to make much of a difference. Also, make sure you don't bury your wires until you have made adjustments to the lighting at night. I like to install my timers inside my home or in the backyard behind a locked gate where no one can get to them. One other hint, when you install lights make sure at least one light is installed under each window of your home. That way if someone tries to get in, he'll be seen.

In high-risk areas, I like to use a lot of plants, such as agaves, cacti and bougainvillea. Plant these under windows and in dark corners where someone could hide. Most are easy to take care of and require little water and maintenance. Trees that I like to use are acacias, mesquite and Texas ebony. Again, all of these require little water and maintenance.

Pruning your shrubs and trees are the most important things you can do to reduce the chances of your home being burglarized. Make sure you reduce all your shrubs to a size that would be difficult to hide behind. Also, trim your trees so that you can see under them and so no one can hide behind them.

A couple other ideas you might want to try are:

Using 3 to 10 inches of river run in all non-pathways. It is virtually impossible to walk on without spraining an ankle.

Shining your low-voltage lights away from windows, but onto the backside of trees and shrubs. This will create beauty and privatize your home at the same time.

Keeping your lawn maintained. Don't allow the grass to grow high, shrubs to grow too large or debris to accumulate. An unkempt yard gives the illusion that you are out of town.

Mosquitoes

If you thought things couldn't get any more uncomfortable in this muggy weather, think again. Mosquitoes are about to descend on the valley. Actually, they're going to be rising up in swarms from the pools of stagnant water that the monsoons bring.

I recently spoke to Dr. Kirk Smith, an entomologist at the University of Arizona Maricopa Agricultural Center, where they do a lot of research on insects. I found out that if you're bitten by a mosquito, you might get more than a red, itchy spot. Smith said mosquitoes can carry diseases like encephalitis, dengue fever (both are prevalent in Arizona), yellow fever and even malaria. They can also transmit heartworm to dogs and cats.

There are some simple steps you can take to prevent mosquito infestations around your home, office and schools:

Change stagnant water in pet dishes, birdbaths and kiddie pools often.
Make sure your potted plants have good drainage.
Remove anything in your yard that has the potential to collect water.

There are also organic ways to control mosquitoes. I've had success with the following:

To trap mosquitoes, sprinkle instant coffee or mineral oil on standing water to trap mosquitoes.
Blend 1-1/2 cups basil leaves with 1 quart water; strain into a spray bottle and mist the affected area.
Mix finely crushed garlic with water; strain into a spray bottle and mist the affected area.

Some plants will repel mosquitoes. Try planting these in your yard:

Artemesia
Bachelor's Button
Basil

There is one tool out there that gets rid of bugs that I think is a bad idea. Electric bug zappers sizzle critters to a crisp and usually kill more good bugs than bad ones. *You know how much I love beneficial insects.*

The heat and humidity are bad enough without adding bug attacks to the mix. Use natural and organic methods of pest control whenever you can and your efforts will go a long way toward making your summer more bearable.

For more information about bugs, visit *ag.arizona.edu.*

Organic Produce

I love to grow my own organic fruits and vegetables, but sometimes even I need to run to the store for some last-minute ingredients. And when I do, it can be tough to find organic produce at the supermarket.

To qualify as organic, produce must contain at least 95 percent organically produced ingredients, so check the sticker. Those fruits and vegetables that are not grown organically will usually have a lot of chemicals added to them for a number of reasons such as pest and disease control or to make them ripen faster. In some cases, chemicals are used to slow the rate of ripening to make sure they don't go bad before being purchased at the grocery store.

Now, if you can't grow your own or find the organic stuff in the store, there are still some things to do that will limit your intake of dangerous chemicals. Here are some tips and information about some of the produce at risk of being highly contaminated with chemicals:

Cucumbers: The skin holds most of the chemicals, so always peel cucumbers. In a recent survey of the most contaminated food, cucumbers were 12th worst out of 42 common vegetables.

Strawberries: The farther away from the strawberry patch, the more chemicals growers have to spray to make the berry last. Try to buy locally grown berries. And don't forget to rinse your strawberries under cool, running water before eating.

Spinach: The chemicals used on spinach can interfere with hormone production and might even cause cancer. Because chemicals can get trapped in dense leaves, carefully wash each and every leaf under cool, running water.

Apples: More pesticides are used on apples grown in the United States than almost any other fruit or vegetable. Even after washing them, always peel your apples.

Cantaloupes: These melons often contain 5 of the longest-lasting chemicals, some of which are banned, but still can be found in the soil. Before cutting, wash the outside of the melon - putting a knife through the unwashed rind will contaminate the part you eat.

Grapes: These ripen so fast that mold tends to become the growers' largest problem. To solve this problem, growers and transporters spray 17 chemicals to help preserve the grapes. Always wash grapes under cool, running water before eating. *Note: Never buy grapes grown outside the United States. Other countries, especially Chile, use a lot of incredibly harsh chemicals.*

Green Beans: There are more than 60 types of pesticides that growers use on green beans. If possible, grow your own. If you do need to buy them, always buy fresh beans and don't forget to wash them thoroughly.

Warning: Broccoli, watermelon, green onion, plums and bananas usually contain the most harmful chemicals.

Good News: Avocado, sweet corn, onion, sweet potatoes and cauliflower are usually the least chemically harmful.

Remember, fruits and vegetables grow well here in the southwest, so grow your own to make sure they are chemical free.

Pets And Your Garden

If you're like me, pets are a part of your family and you go out of your way to make sure they are well cared for. In the garden, though, you have to be careful - some plants, fertilizers and pesticides commonly used in and around many homes can actually hurt our 4-legged friends.

Always check with your nursery to make sure the fertilizers and pesticides you're using are not poisonous, but don't forget to check the toxicity of the plants you're purchasing, as well. There are many, but I've listed the most common types of harmful plants found in the southwest.

Amaryllis: The bulbs are poisonous.

Azalea: The leaves and the nectar from the flowers contain glycoside, a potentially powerful poison that strikes the heart of humans and animals. It can cause nausea, a burning sensation in the mouth and prickly feeling on the skin. Native Americans from Delaware once used this as a suicide potion.

Calla Lily: All parts of this plant are poisonous.

Dieffenbachia: This plant contains strychnine, which will burn the mouth and can paralyze vocal cords.

English Ivy: This plant's leaves and berries are poisonous.

Iris: The iris' underground stem is poisonous.

Lantana: All parts of lantana are poisonous, and the green berries are especially toxic.

Oleander: All parts of the oleander are extremely poisonous. If you burn the clippings, the plant will even release poisonous fumes.

Philodendron: Some varieties will cause skin rashes, but all varieties are poisonous.

Rubber Plant: The rubber plant's milky sap is poisonous.

Spathiphyllum (Peace Lily): The Peace Lily's flowers, leaves and stem are poisonous.

To deter your pets from nibbling on a poisonous plant, apply a light layer of Tabasco sauce or cayenne pepper around the plants in question. Additionally, spread citrus peels or rose stem clippings around the plants you want your pet to avoid.

There are worries, other than how your pets interact with garden plants, that can come from your back yard. For instance, mosquitoes are a big concern right now. Some types can carry heartworm, encephalitis and the dengue virus.

Sitting water from monsoon storms provides a great breeding ground for mosquitoes. Bacillus thuringiensis israelensis (Bti) is an organic way to prevent mosquito babies from being born. For more information, visit *www.Arbico.com.*

Additionally, when it comes to preventing fleas and ticks, the toxins in most products can cause more health problems than any little bug. The best thing is to go organic. To try the organic approach to warding off fleas and ticks, try the following plants and remedies:

Plant artemisia and santolina.

Shampoo your pet with shampoo that contains tea tree oil.

Treat your pet to a citrus shampoo with D-Limonene in it.

Place eucalyptus or cedar bark in the garden or in your pet's bed.

Dust outside areas of concern with food-grade diatomaceous earth (food grade only). The dust slices fleas and ticks so they dehydrate and die. Inside, spread diatomaceous earth on your rugs, then vacuum.

Remember that organic and natural remedies will undoubtedly be the best way to handle problems with pests, weeds and soil.

Water
- Deeply and infrequently.

Prune
- Summer flowering perennials need spent blooms removed.
- Surface tree roots need to be removed but no more than 20% of the root system per year.
- Wisterias that failed to bloom need the roots pruned.

Fertilize
- Use organic fertilizer on all planting areas (10 - 20 lbs./1,000 sq. ft.); especially peppers and tomatoes.
- All planting areas and lawns need to be foliar fed with Extreme Juice.

Pest Control
- Treat grub worms with beneficial nematodes.
- Spray bacillus thuringiensis for cabbage loopers on cauliflower, broccoli, cabbage and brussel sprouts.
- Garlic tea or water blast takes care of aphids on tender, new fall growth. Adding 2 oz. molasses to gallon of spray is better.
- Release ladybugs.
- Dust fire ant mounds with diatomaceous earth then release beneficial nematodes.
- Black spot and powdery mildew on roses can be treated with Extreme Juice plus 1 cup skim milk per gallon of spray.

- Kill white flies with insecticidal soap.
- If plants are suffering from iron chlorosis use chelated iron and sulfur, or Texas Greensand.

Plant

- Remember plant your wildflower seeds if you haven't already- you have from late September to early November.
- By early September finish warm season lawn grass planting.
- Time to transplant established spring flowering bulbs - iris, daylilies.
- Perennials.
- Cool season grasses and leafy root crops - carrots, turnips, beets.

Odds 'n Ends

- Leave grass clippings on lawn when you do your weekly mowing.
- Turn the compost pile.
- Remove bad fruit on citrus.
- Start refrigerating tulips and hyacinth bulbs.

September

Autumn Flowers And Vegetables

It's that time of year to start planting and you will find a lot of different types of flowers and vegetables in your local nursery. These are typically sold by seed or in small pony packs.

I find that some types of flowers and vegetables are hard to transplant and would rather be planted from seed. You need to start planting from seed right now because as our weather cools down, the soil will cool down, which slows down or completely stops the germination process.

It's tricky to get seeds germinated, but a few suggestions are:

Looking for the "packed for season" date which will tell you when the seed packet was meant to be planted.

Not purchasing any seeds that have been stored outdoors. Make sure the seed rack is located indoors before purchasing and do not leave them in the hot vehicle while you do more shopping. Take them home and store them in the refrigerator (a Ziploc bag makes a good container) until you are ready to use them.

Always wash your hands well after handling seeds. A lot of seeds are covered with fungicides, which could be poisonous.

Make sure to keep the area moist until the seed germinates. If the area dries out, the seed or plants will die.

Some of the flowers and vegetables I like to plant include: cosmos, alyssum, sweet pea, sunflowers, marigolds, California poppy, gaillardia, black-eyed Susan, nasturtium, zinnia, larkspurs, squash, beets, watermelon, cucumber, radish, carrots, cowpeas, sweet corn and snap peas. Bachelor buttons love un-amended soil and very little fertilizer.

Bulbs

Bulbs to a lot of people are a mysterious element of gardening that scares a lot of folks into not planting them. But believe it or not, they are one of the easiest types of flowers to grow as long as you do a couple of things to help these babies out.

One of the first and foremost important items to remember is to prepare the soil. Most of our soils are high in clay and hold moisture, which is the biggest enemy of bulbs. They like well-drained, rich soil in a neutral pH range, which means that the bulbs should be placed in well-composted soil - raised beds are perfect too - and each bulb should be placed on a bed of sand 4 to 5 inches deep. My favorite way to install bulbs is to remove approximately 12 inches of soil and add sand to the depth desired for each bulb. Place the bulb directly on top of the sand and then add 1/2 peat moss to 1/2 indigenous soil. While you are backfilling, add plenty of soft phosphate and blood meal. One more general rule for bulb planting is to plant the bulb at approximately 1/2 of the recommended depth so if the package recommends 4 inches, here in the southwest you'll only want to plant at 2 inches. Planting them too deeply delays blooming in the spring.

Some flowers need to have cold weather to produce and bloom. Because we don't get the chill that is necessary, we need to place tulips, hyacinth and crocus in the refrigerator for 6 to 8 weeks starting now. Place the bulbs in a paper bag and store in the vegetable compartment. One more hint, make sure you don't have any fruits or vegetables around the bulbs or you may possibly stunt or kill the bulbs.

Some of my favorite bulbs are:

Paperwhites which belong to the narcissus family. They are easy to grow outside or inside and they are a great flower for holiday color. I plant them in a bowl filled with gravel. Plant the bulbs pointed-side up, then fill the container with water. Maintain this level at all times. Place in a cool location inside your home. Early morning sunlight is ideal. Within 4 to 6 weeks, you will have a profusion of blooms. Of course, you can just go out and plant your paperwhites in the soil as long as you follow my directions. Animals should not eat anything in the narcissus family because they are considered poisonous.

Freesias are another one of my favorite bulbs that not only look good but also make a great cut flower for   indoor. They do need afternoon shade and have a great fragrance, especially when planted around small patio areas.

Crocus will need to be chilled as described above and grow into a beautiful sea of flowers if planted densely enough. Make sure to plant them in areas that get afternoon shade and in front of any other tall growth.

Ranunculus a long-lasting flower you can plant for spring color. Make sure to soak the bulb in water overnight and if you want, add a little dash of liquid seaweed for good measure.

Bearded Iris is not a bulb, but it is time to divide them. You can purchase the rhizomes right now. Plant them in a sunny location just below the soil surface. Does wonderfully well here in our lower deserts with afternoon shade. Remember to plant your bulbs and rhizomes in drifts of 10 or more for a more dramatic effect.

Fall Gardening Fun

We are coming up on the most productive time of year for gardening in the southwest.

The first thing to remember is that the soil needs a lot of organic material. This makes for a richer, more productive, chemical-free garden. To achieve good soil, lay down a 6 inch layer of compost, then add blood meal and soft phosphate along with volcanite (about 5 pounds per 50 square feet). Use a hard rake and a pick to work the products about 12 inches into the soil.

If you don't want the backbreaking work of tilling the soil, just build a raised garden about 12 to 18 inches high. Fill it with pure compost or an organic planting mix.

To reap the benefits of your work, plant tomatoes, cucumbers, squash and black-eyed peas immediately. When the weather cools down (usually at the end of September), plant winter vegetables like artichokes, bush beans, carrots, garlic, lettuce, onions, peas, radishes, spinach and strawberries.

To increase your chances of success in the garden, plant companion plants like thyme, mint, lavender and alyssum throughout your garden. These plants are all natural insect repellants and humans love their smell and taste.

Remember: If you plant anything by seed, you must keep that seed moist until it germinates. A dry seed is a dead seed.

Watering rule: Be sure the water penetrates at least 6 inches into the ground each time you water. And make sure to cover the surrounding soil with 2 to 4 inches of mulch.

Fertilizing tip: Keep it organic! Fish emulsion and liquid seaweed or my Extreme Juice are wonderful fertilizers. When the weather gets cooler, try mixing a little liquid humate into your fertilizer. It will break things down and make it easier for plant roots to absorb the nutrients.

Fall Lawn Care: Overseeding

Daytime temperatures are still warm, but those night and early morning temperatures are nice and cool. That means it's time to change the grass.

For those of you just moving into the valley, it's probably news to you that there are two lawns: summer and winter. If you want a green lawn in the winter, you'll need to plant it soon; and your window to do it only lasts from now until November.

The advantages of overseeding include weed control, nut grass control and a green lawn for 6 to 9 months.

For a lush green lawn, there are some tasks to be completed and timing is important. See the steps below for an easy how-to list for creating a beautiful winter lawn:

Eight Weeks to Go: De-thatch (July or August)

This process removes grass and other material that builds up in the soil, blocking out light, oxygen and water. If you can see the soil through your grass, there is no need to de-thatch. If you can't see the soil below your grass, de-thatch your lawn 8 weeks before overseeding.

Four Weeks to Go: Stop Fertilizing Your Lawn

Do not fertilize your lawn again until you see grass sprouting.

Two Weeks to Go: Adjust Your Lawnmower

Start lowering your mower blade and cut your Bermuda grass with normal frequency.

One Week to Go: Reduce Watering Time

Cut the watering time in half to slow growth.

Overseeding Day:

Mow grass normally, then drop the mower and scalp the Bermuda grass. Rake away the excess grass, then aerate your lawn (you can rent an aerating machine from a local rental shop).

After you've aerated the lawn, use a drop spreader or whirlybird to spread your grass seeds in a criss-cross pattern across your lawn. Unless you recently put in sod, I recommend using only perennial rye seed. Now, this seed is more expensive, but uses less water, doesn't stain clothes, creates a lush lawn and requires less mowing.

The seed-to-lawn ratio is about 20 pounds of seed for every 1,000 square feet of lawn.

After you've spread the grass seed, spread a 1/4 to 1/2 inch layer of compost over the seed. Don't apply the compost too heavily or you'll suffocate the seed.

Remember: A dry seed is a dead seed. Water your new lawn 3 to 4 times each day, in 3 to 5 minute increments. Keep the soil moist, but not wet (i.e., no standing water).

Allow the grass to grow 2 inches, then stop watering your lawn for 24 hours. Mow your lawn, then set up a new watering schedule.

Note: Always water in the morning and fertilize regularly with organics.

Herbs That Heal

Planting an herb garden is going to do a lot for you besides add tasty ingredients to your food. Herbs can help heal many of the problems that ail you.

For centuries, farmers, gardeners, herbalists and scientists have grown and developed herbs to help people feel better. They are a source of vitamins and are still used to a great extent in Europe and Asia.

Even now, pharmaceutical companies study herbs and the benefits they can bring to humans. Herbs are base ingredients in everything from aspirin and cancer-fighting drugs to cosmetics.

Here is a list of common plants and herbs that can help cure what ails you.

Aloe: Apply to sunburned skin.

Calendula: Steep petals in boiling water, then soak a compress in the liquid and use on minor cuts and burns.

Feverfew: To cure a headache, place a feverfew leaf between two slices of bread, then eat.

Garlic: To cure a mild cold or sore throat, drink a mixture of crushed garlic cloves with hot water. Raw garlic can also help fight bronchial infections.

Lemon Balm or Onion: Place crushed lemon balm leaves or slices of onion on an insect bite to reduce the itchiness.

Mint Tea: To soothe a stomachache, drink a cup of mint tea.

Parsley: To fight bad breath, chew on a few sprigs of parsley. Alternatively, you can mix a handful of chopped parsley with two tablespoons of water and use the mixture as a hair tonic. It will simulate your hair follicles and make your scalp feel great.

Peppermint: To soothe a cough, drink tea made of peppermint leaves and hot water.

Vinca Major: To stop a cut from bleeding, apply a few leaves to the wound.

To get herbs to grow healthy, plant them in a white 1 or 5 gallon plastic bucket in organic soil (1 part perlite, 1 part vermiculite, 1 part potting soil and a handful of compost).

Place the potted herbs in an eastern exposure where they will receive morning light and afternoon shade. Fertilize your herbs with a light dose of fish emulsion, liquid seaweed or Extreme Juice every 3 weeks or so.

Our water has a lot of salt in it, so when you irrigate, make sure the water flushes out of the bottom of the pot.

WARNING: If you are pregnant or taking medications, talk to your doctor before using any of these remedies.

Kill Unwanted Insects With Homemade Concoctions

If your home and plants have been bombarded with unwanted bugs, you don't need to run to the store to purchase harmful or expensive chemical sprays. Often, you can create homemade concoctions with products already in your cupboard.

Inside Ant Killer: Combine even amounts of rue (an herb), bay and cinnamon and set the combination in places where ant traffic is heaviest.

Boric Acid Balls: Combine 1 tsp. boric acid, 1/2 cup flour, 1/2 cup water and 1/2 cup sugar. To get rid of cockroaches and ants, set the balls where these insects are most prevalent.

Fungicide on Plants: Combine 3 tsp. apple cider vinegar, 1 gallon of water and banana peels. Pour the concoction in a spray bottle and spray your indoor plants.

Fly Killer: To kill flies, grind garlic in a cup and mix with a small amount of water. Use as a spray.

General Insect Killer: Blend 2 cups tomato leaves, 1/2 tsp. dishwashing liquid and 1 quart water. Put the concoction in a spray bottle and spray unwanted pests.

Citrus Peels for Ants: Grind citrus peels, mix with water and pour on ant mounds.

Ant Trap: Mix boric acid with peanut butter and spread on cardboard. Place cardboard in high-traffic areas to control ants.

Note: Keep concoctions out of the reach of children.

Organic Vegetable Gardens

Over the next few weeks, it will be time to start that organic vegetable garden. You can't beat the taste of fresh vegetables out of your garden and growing them is easy, especially during our warm days and cool nights.

To start your garden, make sure to find a place with plenty of morning sun - 4 to 6 hours - and afternoon shade. I build my gardens no wider than 4 feet across and 12 feet long. I also mix in plenty of organic material, including:

> *Four to six bags compost*
> *Four to six bags manure*
> *One 5 pound bag blood meal*
> *One 5 pound bag soft phosphate*

Blend this combination into the soil approximately 12 to 15 inches deep and let it cook for at least two weeks before planting.

Some of the fruits and vegetables I like to plant include:

Strawberries: Don't wait. Start right now. Buy the Chandler-Sequoia varieties for the best results. Keep them warm during the winter with a clear 4 foot plastic green house structure made from rebar or PVC pipe. Cool strawberries during the summer with grapevines trained to grow over the top of the strawberries. Remember to plant strawberries in deep soil and don't plant them next to mint, rosemary or thyme, but they love beans, lettuce and spinach as neighbors.

Tomatoes: Grow them in the fall and if you plant them early, plant ripening varieties, sometimes called short-season varieties. Some of these go by names such as Early Girl, Roma, Celebrity or Pearson. Tomatoes love even, consistent water, mulch in the soil and fish emulsion every 2 weeks. Frost protection is necessary for late-ripening varieties. Do not plant tomatoes near fennel, pepper or eggplants. Always remember to rotate tomato placement every year to keep soil healthy.

Peppers: Take about the same amount of care with peppers and space your plants about 12 to 18 inches apart in enriched, well-drained soil. Don't let them dry out. Afternoon shade is a necessity. Apply fish emulsion every 2 weeks and an occasional dose of blood meal works well, too. Plant them next to sage and tarragon and remember they will grow over the winter if protected from the frost. Try planting them in a pot and moving them into a sheltered area when frost threatens.

A couple of things to remember with any type of vegetable is to go with the shortest-season variety you can find. Plant in well-drained and well-prepared soil. Stay organic by using fish emulsion, cottonseed meal and as much compost as you can afford to buy. One more thing, never use dangerous pesticides or fertilizers in your garden.

Wildflowers

Around this time of year, the nights are cool and the days are warm and that means it's time to seed our homes with desert wildflowers. They survive in our soils with little water and an occasional dose of fish emulsion.

Once established, a lot of desert wildflowers reseed themselves readily and are a great way to add spring and fall colors with little or no work. There are approximately 90 species of desert wildflowers, a lot of which are used for attracting birds and butterflies. They also attract a lot of beneficial insects that will help with pollination and pest control, which keeps with my philosophy of staying organic.

I throw my wildflowers into vacant yards, garden areas, roadways and anywhere I feel a burst of color is needed, kind of like the Johnny Appleseed of wildflowers. They will grow virtually anywhere.

To plant your wildflowers, find an area that is in full sun. Prepare your soil by loosening the soil to approximately 6 to 8 inches and then rake the soil smooth, removing the dirt clods. Once you have the soil loose, mix your seeds with a little sand and start to cast the seeds onto the surface of the soil. Rake the seeds into the soil, making sure these seeds are covered with 1/8 to 1/4 inch of soil. Start watering the seeds 3 to 4 times weekly until the seeds surface, then cut back the watering to 1 time per week. I also give my wildflowers a dose of fish emulsion once a month for an extra burst of growth and great blooms. You may need to cover your wildflowers with netting to keep the birds off until they are established. Some of my favorites include:

Desert Marigolds
California Poppies
Gaillardia
Penstemon
Shirley Poppies
Mexican Hat
Desert Bluegrass
Spreading Fleabane
Lupine

To order your wildflowers, call Wild Seed Inc., at (602) 276-3536 or Desert Botanical Gardens.

October

Calendar for Organic Gardening

Water
- Deeply and infrequently, still!!

Prune
- Trees need dead and damaged wood removed.
- As needed pick - prune shrubs. Save major trimming for winter.

Fertilize
- Mulch all bare soil and add new material to top of all exposed existing mulch.
- All plantings and lawns need to be foliar fed with Extreme Juice.

Pest Control
- Spray bacillus thuringiensis for cabbage loopers in your garden. Then release trichogramma wasps.

Plant
- Cool season vegetables.
- Bulbs in well-drained soil.
- Finish all wildflower planting.
- Cool season grasses.
- Trees, shrubs, vines.
- Spring and summer flowering perennials.

- Cool season flowers: English daisies, wall flowers, garlic, kale, flowering cabbage, pinks, snapdragons, violas, pansies, Iceland poppies.
- Strawberries.

Odds 'n Ends

- Use partially completed compost for top-dressing mulch around ornamentals and vegetables.
- Prepare new planting beds using completed compost.
- Turn old compost and build new compost piles.
- Leave grass clippings on lawn as you mow weekly.
- All bare soil needs mulching.
- Plant sweet peas now. Let them trellis for great spring blooms.
- Overseed Bermuda lawns.

October

Backyard Composting

By choosing to compost, you have taken a large step in reducing the solid waste stream, reusing valuable organic resources right from home and recycling their rich nutrients by returning them to the soil, thereby enriching your little corner of the earth.

Compost is the resulting product of the natural decomposition process of organic matter. It is an excellent way to recycle organic matter or dead plant material. What begins as household organic materials becomes compost - a dark, crumbly, sweet-smelling, humus-rich soil enrichment.

When introduced into gardens and flower beds your homegrown compost:

- significantly increases the soil's ability to combat diseases and environmental and seasonal hardships;
- boosts the nutrients upon which plants depend to survive and flourish;
- improves the soil structure, allowing oxygen into the soil by loosening clay-like soil, which promotes healthy root growth;

- helps sandy soil to hold more moisture, permitting plants to take stronger root;
- helps prevent soil erosion and improves moisture retention.

All this is accomplished without expensive additives or chemicals.

Backyard composter kits include composter, a starter supply of mulch and instructions and are available at the following Phoenix locations:

Skunk Creek Landfill
3165 W. Happy Valley Road - (602) 262-7109
Monday - Friday, 5:30 am - 5 pm
Saturday - Sunday, 8 am - 4 pm

27th Avenue Solid Waste Management Facility
3060 S. 27th Ave. - (602) 262-6598
Monday - Friday, 5:30 am - 5 pm
Saturday, 8 am - 4 pm

Information provided by the City of Phoenix

Container Gardens

As it cools down, getting a little color in your garden is next to impossible. But, the best way to satisfy your craving is to grow your own annuals in containers.

Some of my favorite types of containers are everything from whiskey barrels to hanging baskets. In the winter, anything will work and during the cool months, you don't need to worry about watering every day.

First, let's talk a little about what type of soil to put in your pots. I like to blend my own special type of potting mix. Try this combination for a soil mix:

1/3 peat moss
1/3 vermiculate
1/3 perlite
1/3 potting soil

Add about 1/4 cup to 1/2 cup of blood meal and 1/4 cup to 1/2 cup soft phosphate. You can also add a pinch of steer manure for an extra punch.

Mix this combination and add some Soil Moist. (Most Fry's Marketplaces carry this product.) This mixture creates a well drained, fertile medium that most flowers love.

Next, find a container, any container will work, but you need a lot of drainage, and the only way to get this is with a lot of holes. The holes must be on the lower side of the container, not on the bottom where the holes can be blocked by debris. For a hanging basket, try lining the wire basket with Spanish moss and then fill it with the above soil mixture.

I use a lot of different types of flowers, but some take the shade a lot better than others.

In the winter, plant in a place that gets afternoon shade because it is where your flowers will last longer in the next year's spring and summer seasons. **A few flowers you might want to try are:**

Primrose: blooms best in cold temperatures.
Freesia: produces a lot of scent; plant from bulbs.
Stock: a great cut flower; produces a lot of scent; pinch back leader for a lot of color.
Geraniums: likes their roots to get a little congested.

Flowers that do well in the shade are:

Begonias: long-lived and sometimes will turn perennial.
Iceland Poppies: one of my favorite types of flowers.
Petunias: are great but make sure you rotate them; sometimes they share diseases with *vincas.*
Alyssum: reseeds easily and grows with little care. Plant on the edge of your pots for a cascading type of effect.

For full-sun areas, try a few of the following:

Nasturtiums: do better planted from seed. Skip the blood meal and bone meal; don't fertilize.
Sweet Peas: grow on a trellis or you can purchase bush types. Plant from seed now for spring blooms, use a trellis for climbing types.
Marigolds: attract a lot of beneficials.
Cosmos: grow better from seed; don't fertilize.
Salvias: like to occasionally be pinched back.
Calendula: should be pinched back often. The flowers look great as a garnish on salads.
Petunias: can also be planted in full sun.

Remember, except for a few varieties, most flowers like an occasional dose of fish emulsion or my Extreme Juice, which has fish emulsion in it. Experiment and you will find growing flowers in pots during the winter is a great remedy for those dull winter blues!

Cool Weather Tips

With the cool weather this season brings, you might like to put together a list of tips that will help avoid problems in the future. First, cut back on watering. Anytime we get one inch or more of rain, you can turn off your system.

Here are some watering guidelines for this of year.

Trees: Water every 14 to 30 days for desert varieties and every 7 to 14 days for high-water use trees. Make sure the water penetrates 3 feet deep with your soil probe.

Shrubs: Water every 14 to 30 days for desert types and 7 to 10 days for high-water use types. Make sure your water penetrates at least 2 feet with your soil probe.

Ground Covers and Vines: Water every 7 to 10 days for desert types and every 7 to 19 days for high-water use. Make sure your water penetrates 1 foot deep with your soil probe.

Wildflowers: If you have wildflower seeds, make sure that they stay damp until they germinate and that they get at least 1 inch of water per month until late January or February. A little fish emulsion helps too.

Annuals: They need water at least every 3 to 7 days to a depth of 6 to 12 inches.

Rye Grass: Make sure your new rye grass lawn stays damp until it comes up and gets to a height of 2 inches. Then cut back on watering to every 3 to 5 days. The water should penetrate to a depth of 8 to 12 inches. Remember, water only in the morning.

Additional water is needed for new planting in sandy soil or extremely hot weather. Remember to water 1-1/2 times beyond the tree or plant canopy.

Some other hints for a cool season of gardening include:

Make sure that you occasionally change the soil in your pots and scrub the pots with a mixture of 1 part bleach and 10 parts water. Soil harbors pathogens and tends to build up after a couple of years of use.

Hold off pruning any frost-tender shrubs.

Fertilizing now will encourage soft growth that is prone to frost damage.

Always cut rye grass with a sharp blade and make sure to mow your lawn only when the grass is dry. This will stress the grass less and help your lawn. Mowers run smoother and create less pollution.

Right now, you may want to check your tangerine trees to see if they are ripe. Color is not an indication of ripeness, so if they are green, they may be ready to eat. In the following couple of weeks, you will want to check your lemons and limes, as well.

Companion Planting

What is companion planting? I can tell you that it's an essential aspect to any successful landscape, and it's really easy to create. Simply put, companion planting is putting plants together that help one another to grow and thrive. This type of gardening will help ward off pests and diseases, as well as strengthen the overall health in your garden. You can also attract "good" pests with certain plants and create polycultures. It's like building a little community where plants grow together, just like in nature.

Like all gardening, companion plants have seasons. Here are some cool-weather companion plants to combine from now until the end of November:

Beets:
  Cabbage
  Lettuce
  Onions

Bok choy:
  Beets
  Chamomile
  Dill
  Onions
  Sage

Broccoli:
  Beets
  Carrots
  Dill
  Marigolds
  Onions
  Rosemary
  Sage

Garlic:
  Beets
  Lettuce
  Tomatoes

Lettuce:
  Beets
  Cabbage
  Carrots
  Cucumbers
  Kale
  Leeks
  Marigolds
  Strawberries
  Radishes *(plant near lettuce to deter aphids)*

Onions:
  Beets
  Lettuce
  Strawberries
  Tomatoes

Radishes:
(these grow under the dirt and tend to repel ants)
  Squash
  Cucumbers
  Peas
  Lettuce *(helps radishes grow strong)*
  Nasturtium
  Melons

Plant cucumbers with sunflowers and you will grow sweeter cucumbers. Do not plant onions near peppers, beans or peas. Planting chamomile among onions will improve the flavor of the onion. Chamomile is also known to improve the health of nearby plants.

The synergy between some plants can be unusual but amazing and the results you get from planting in a companion atmosphere will be outstanding.

Fall Blooms

Fall has arrived and now is your chance to see some of Arizona's most beautiful plants in full bloom. Here is a list of plants that bloom late into the fall season:

Pineleaf Milkweed: This plant is a small shrub with white flowers that attracts butterflies. It can be planted in the sun or partial shade.

Salvia Coccinea: This red-flowered plant is a member of the mint family and attracts hummingbirds. It blooms in the spring, summer and fall, but dies in cold weather.

Hummingbird Bush or California Fuchsia: Blooming in both summer and fall, this orange-flowered plant attracts hummingbirds and needs full sun or partial shade. It can be planted in moist or dry soils and dies in cold weather.

Salvia Leucantha: This Mexican bush sage blooms with purple flowers in late summer and fall. It also attracts hummingbirds.

Maximilian Sunflower: A plant that needs staking, this sunflower blooms in the fall to 5 or 6 feet and attracts solitary bees as well as bumblebees, who feed on the seed heads.

Wild Sunflower: Bumblebees, solitary bees and finches feed on the seed heads of this fall bloomer.

Desert Milkweed: Blooming with white/cream flowers, this plant is loved by butterflies and big tarantula wasps. It also gets bright orange-colored aphids that do not need to be controlled.

Orange Jubilee: This large shrub (up to 10 feet tall) attracts hummingbirds and bumble bees. It blooms in the late spring, summer and fall.

Baja Fairy Duster: Hummingbirds, many different butterflies, solitary bees, quail and dove love to eat the seeds from this plant.

Autumn Sage: Hummingbirds are attracted to this plant, which blooms with pink, red and white flowers on and off nearly all year.

Lantana: This plant comes in all colors and attracts many butterflies.

Eupatorium Greggi "Boothill": Butterflies love this blue-flowered plant, especially when planted in light shade. Butterflies never leave this type of plant.

The Eupatorium greggi "Boothill", is one of my favorites; I think it is the very best fall bloom. This low and spreading plant has lavender-blue flowers that attract butterflies all day long. My butterflies, especially the gulf fritillaries, love it. The gulf fritillary is a friendly butterfly that will settle on your finger.

Look for butterflies in the early mornings and late afternoons. I like to call this time the "glow time," when the light is soft and golden.

Hummingbirds will fly by all day long and will check you out if you wear red.

Hummingbirds are great insect eaters and are also nectar sippers.

Flowers

Here are a few popular flowers and their features:

Chrysanthemums:

They like moist soil. Water 1 to 2 inches per week.

They are heavy feeders.

They will keep from year to year on eastern exposure.

Don't plant near streetlights or cover them at night. They like 12 hours of darkness to bloom.

Snapdragons:

Grow well in containers.

Need well-drained soil.

Sow seeds shallow (seeds need light to germinate).

Pinch back plant to encourage bushy growth.

Do not let them go to seed.

Staking is needed on larger plants.

Spray leaves with fish emulsion.

Petunias:

Need full sun.

Easy to germinate.

Plant with plastic over the tray.
When purchasing, buy them in six-packs without flowers.
They do best in early spring.

Pansies:
Edible.
They grow in rich soil.
Plant in a well-drained area.
Look for deep green leaves.
Need temperatures below 85 degrees.
Pinch back often.

Marigolds:
Edible.
They like warm weather and hot locations.
Shade in the morning is OK.
They will reseed.
Water 1 inch weekly.
Feed monthly.

Geraniums:
Scented plants are edible.
Dappled afternoon shade is OK.
Bloom better if slightly pot bound.
Let the soil dry between watering.
Do not get water on the leaves.

Begonias:
They like light shade.
Do not get water on the leaves.

Alyssum:
Reseed to withstand drought.
Cut back every 4 weeks.
They like full sun.
They like high-alkaline soil, such as the desert soil in Arizona.

Flowers I Love To Plant From Seed

With the weather finally cooling down, you want to start putting in your wildflower seeds. I get a lot of my seeds from the Desert Botanical Gardens or Wild Seed.

Remember, you will get more bloom and healthier plants if you prepare your soil in advance. Till the soil 6 to 8 inches deep and add some bone meal, 5 lbs. per 100 square feet. Also, add a cubic foot bag of compost per 20 to 40 square feet and work it into the top several inches of the soil. I like to seed the following:

Zinnias: attract a lot of butterflies.
Cosmos: attract a lot of birds.
Shirley poppies: attract birds and reseed easily.
Alyssum: attracts a lot of pollinators, such as solitary bees and moths.
Gaillardia: is a great summer bloomer and vigorous re-seeder.
Sweet peas: are fragrant. Allow it to climb or trail over the fence.
Coreopsis: attracts butterflies.
Johnny Jump-ups: provide low border color for cool weather.
Black-eyed Susan: will take over if you are not careful.
Bachelor Buttons: are easy to grow.
California poppies, lupines and flaxes: can be planted on native soil with a layer of mulch applied on the top.

Remember to water every day until the plants are approximately 1 to 2 inches tall and then slowly reduce the water until they start blooming. You will get more blooms if the plants are slightly stressed for water during their bloom cycle. Most of the plants will reseed if you leave them alone after the blooming cycle.

Organic Gardening

Organic gardening is good for the environment and your plants.

Using natural fertilizer, such as manure, worm castings, chicken droppings, bat guano or peatmoss, helps enrich the soil. With organic gardening, you're letting the soil fertilize the plants. It takes two years to get good soil.

Oxygen in the soil causes roots to be able to penetrate deeper, resist diseases and grow better. Introduce air into the soil with aeration, digging approximately 2 shovels-full deep.

Spray plants with liquid seaweed to help protect against frost damage. Fish emulsion, molasses and hydrogen peroxide all help plants resist diseases.

Encourage life and bio-diversity by introducing ladybugs, lace wings, beneficial wasps and earthworms.

Worms are easy to grow in Arizona and they help the environment. Worm castings are great fertilizers and terrific soil amenders. They eat grass clippings, eggshells, tea bags, coffee grounds, etc. Worms need to be kept at a temperature of 65 to 75 degrees. I've known people to keep them right by their sinks as garbage disposals.

80 to 90 percent of pesticidal use is by households. You can eliminate that by going all-organic. For example, B.T. kills a lot of non-beneficial bugs such as caterpillars without killing beneficial ones, such as lizards, toads and beneficial insects. Buy it at any nursery or from Arbico. Diatomaceous earth kills ants, crickets, grasshoppers, slugs and roaches. Putting banana peels underneath rose bushes make them resistant to aphids.

A few herbs ward off insects. Some good ones are rue, rosemary, onion, chives, sage, basil, garlic and lavender.

Remember to deep water without getting water on the leaves. Use T-tape, soaker hose or flood irrigation. Drip systems also work well.

Scented Plants

Whenever I landscape a yard, I look for the simple ways to make it more enjoyable for whoever is going to visit. One of the ways is through the use of scented plants. Plants that produce scents can excite, calm and bring back fond memories of the past. In the southwest, we have many types of plants that create these scents. They are easy to grow and are indigenous to our area.

My favorite scent is *jasmine*. It's sweet fragrance works great in the front entry of your home. It's easy to grow and handles shady areas well. Another fragrant jasmine-type plant is *star jasmine* and although not a true jasmine, it has a wonderful fragrance. It works great in shady areas or on the east side of your home where it will receive morning sun.

Lavender is a very fragrant plant, traditionally associated with English gardens. Plant the lavender in sunny areas where it will receive excellent drainage. Wet feet will cause the plant to die from rot. Not only are the blooms intensely fragrant, the flowers are edible and can be used to flavor honey and vinegar. Prune the flower stalks off when the buds begin to open and dry for potpourri.

The *sages* are also fragrant. Plant autumn sage, Mexican bush sage and salvia clevelandii near patios and walkways as they will release fragrance when you brush by them.

Another aromatic plant that does well here in the desert is *rosemary*. Plant it in full sun near sitting areas where you can enjoy its fragrance. Don't forget, it's wonderful grilled with steaks or tossed into spaghetti sauce.

I promised you a few native plants and the first to come to mind is *creosote*. It has a wonderful pine scent, especially after thundershowers. This plant needs full sun and little water once it's established.

Desert lavender is another shrub with fragrant leaves. This native thrives in full sun and will grow 8 feet tall. On a small scale, the autumn sage is a native, as is *white evening primrose*. This evening-blooming plant opens with 3-inch white primroses that are sweetly scented.

One last plant, not used too often, but is perfect in any slightly breezy area is *aloysia*. It has a fantastic honey scent when it's in bloom, which is most of the spring and late summer. This shrubby plant can be eventually trained as a small tree or allowed to grow as a shrub 9 to 10 feet tall.

Roaches

If you see one roach, there are actually hundreds roaming around. Here are some tips to keep them out of your house:

Use caulk, steel wool, copper mesh and wire screens to seal up cracks and crevices. Many people have holes where wires are going into their home. Putting a screen over the holes helps keep roaches and other critters out.

Keep doors and windows closed.

Pour bleach down drains.

Roaches love to live in river rock.

Remove cardboard boxes and paper grocery bags from your home. Never store grocery bags in your house. Roaches love to eat the glue in grocery bags.

Don't let your drains dry out.

Use drain covers in your showers and bathtubs.

Don't leave food or water lying around. Roaches are attracted to both. Many people leave food and water out for their pets, but this is not a good idea.

Stop dripping faucets.

Spread boric acid or diatomaceous earth on the floors inside your house to keep roaches away. You can also make a 50/50 solution of baking soda and sugar, put it in jar lids and leave inside and around your home.

Mix 2 parts flour, 1 part boric acid and 1 part sugar and moisten with a little bit of water to form little cakes. Place the cakes inside and around the house.

Keep the above solutions away from pets and kids.

Salad Gardening in the Southwest

The upcoming cool months are the best months to grow a salad garden. There are a few things you should remember if you want to grow great greens with little to no effort.

Try to plant your garden in any area that will receive afternoon shade. This is important because many greens and edible flowers thrive in the coolness of the morning sun, but don't like the heat of the midday and afternoon sun.

Add a lot of organics to your soil. Nothing, but nothing, can replace good, old-fashioned compost. It's filled with all the nutrients required to grow a garden, especially a winter salad garden. Synthetic fertilizers and other products only upset nature's balance and poison the ground.

Garden soil should be well drained, so dig deep and add a lot of compost.

Salad gardens no longer mean a few wilting leaves of lettuce, radishes and cucumbers. These days, you can plant a wide variety of vegetables, flowers and herbs. All of the plants listed below can be grown in pots or in the ground.

Chard is one of my favorites. Not only is chard delicious, but it's also easy to grow; Bright Light Swiss Chard adds beauty to your garden.

Spinach is another one of those leafy greens that also does well in the southwest desert. It prefers moist soil and partial shade. As with all leafy crops, add a lot of blood meal and steer manure to the soil before you plant spinach. Space plants 10 inches apart, and make sure you plant them only when we're headed into cooler weather.

If you are planting *lettuce* from seed, make sure you refrigerate your seeds 24 to 48 hours prior to planting. Plant them only after cooler weather strikes. Make sure you plant seeds 6 to 14 inches apart. Watch out for aphids, slugs, snails and cut worms.

When planting *carrots,* use compost, not manure, to amend the soil. Plant each plant about 15 inches deep in the soil. A little soft phosphate will help with fertilization needs. *Onions* and *sage* are good companion crops.

To add a little color to your salad garden, you might try planting edible flowers and herbs. Some of my favorites include:

Nasturtium
Basil
Onion
Pansies
Thyme
Parsley

Most importantly, don't use synthetic fertilizers or pesticides on any food products in your garden. Enjoy!

Wildflowers

I love wildflowers. Planting them is so easy and they come up with sunshine and water. Of course, if you like the look of a perfectly manicured yard, this type of gardening might not be for you. But I urge everyone to pick up some wildflower seeds and try them. You can plant them in pots or make a great big meadow in your yard. They add such beauty and color; it's an alluring atmosphere for any area.

You don't have to be an advanced gardener to have this effect. Right now is the best time to plant wildflowers. The cooler temperatures and the winter rain encourage germination of the seed. Plant a few packets of seed in your garden. Once they come up you will be so glad to see the bright splashes of color. Get your wildflower seeds from the Desert Botanical Garden. Their quality and variety provides outstanding results. Not all seeds are equal.

Make sure you plant in an area where you can supply an adequate amount of water. Just in case we don't get enough rain, we need to supplement watering. The seeds need to keep moist and the best way to do this - besides rain - is to use a gentle watering system. If you do it by hand, use a watering can with a lot of holes in the spout so you don't dislodge the seeds. A water wand works well, also. You can pick these items up at your local nursery.

To distribute the seeds evenly when planting, always mix them with potting soil, compost or sand. The ratio should be one part seed to four parts filler. If you put the seeds in too thickly, they will compete too hard for water, sun and possibly other nutrients in the soil, causing a weak, sparse plant.

You can also just throw some seed onto decomposed granite and just gently wash them into contact with the soil. If you plant directly into soil without granite, stir up the surface a bit. Only do this about 1 inch, so as not to stir up any weed seeds which like to hide out to sprout and grow.

Always sow 1/2 of the seed in one direction, and then in another, like a crisscross pattern. After washing them down gently with water, you can help along the germination by pressing them into the soil with the backside of a rake. Remember not to go too deep, though, because they need the sun so vitally.

You can even plant some seeds next to already existing plants and trees that have emitters. You won't have to do much to make these grow, because the circumstance for proper growth has already been established. Water a little more frequently until they start to sprout up a couple of inches and then resume you normal watering schedule.

Planting wildflowers in pots is so easy, too. It creates a variety of color in just the right places you want to place them and, if you buy lightweight pots, you can move them around every so often for variety. It's a beautiful touch to apartment balconies, front porches or anywhere you want to narrow down a nice splash of color.

Weed often, because weeds will compete with your wildflowers for sunshine, water and nutrients. If the wildflowers get too thick, thin them out. This will be sure to give them the right amount of room to grow. I thin them down to one plant every few inches.

Once the wildflowers are up and going, no matter where you've planted them, hit them with a good dose of fish emulsion or my Extreme Juice. You can find Extreme Juice at any Fry's Marketplace.

Often you will find your wildflowers will reseed after being in bloom for approximately 2 weeks. You can let the seed naturally fall or save them to replant, share with a neighbor or start a fresh group elsewhere in your yard. You potentially could have a whole neighborhood with splashes of color throughout, if you all enjoy this simple way of gardening.

There are annual wildflowers as well as perennial. Annuals have to be cut down to ground level once the plants have died back. Leave the roots because they decompose into the soil, which adds nutrients back in as well as aerates the soil. Perennial means they will return year after year. Just cut perennials back to the new growth and keep on growing. The new flowers will soon start sprouting all over again.

I hope you enjoy wildflowers as much as I do.

Winter Flowers

Spring isn't the only time to plant flowers. With the dog days of summer drawing to a close and giving us cooler nights and gorgeous mornings, you can add flowers to your garden and accent your landscape.

To plant flowers this time of year, you'll need to know what type of light the planting areas receive to determine your planting options.

What to Plant and Where:

Shaded Areas: From seed, you can plant delphinium, larkspur, calendula, Icelandic poppies and Shirley Poppies. If you're looking to transplant plants, begonias are a good way to go. As for bulbs, try planting daffodils and narcissus.

Areas With Afternoon Shade: Try planting scented geraniums, alyssum, petunias, lobelias, marigolds, ornamental kale and pansies.

Areas With Full Sun: Try your hand at growing sunflowers, chrysanthemums, lupine, wildflowers, nasturtiums and hollyhocks. Use asparagus as a backdrop to your flower garden.

Once lighting and plants have been determined, prepare the soil to give flowers the best opportunity for success. To do so, put 4 to 6 inches of compost, soft phosphate and blood meal on top of the soil, then rototill the mixture about 12 inches deep.

Mix 1/4 cup of liquid seaweed, 1/4 cup of molasses and 1/4 cup fish emulsion into 3 gallons of water and drench the soil, then plant your flowers.

Add cedar mulch to the top of the soil - this will act as an insect repellant and keep the ground moist.

For an added kick, add paramagnetic lava sand, like Volcanite, according to the directions on the back of the package. This will help flowers grow and blossom.

November

Calendar for Organic Gardening

Water
- Reduce irrigation on established plant material.
- At least every 5 to 10 days on your wildflower beds.

Prune
- Your flowering plants need spent blooms and seed heads removed.
- Remove dead limbs from trees before leaves fall.
- Now is the time for major tree pruning.

Fertilize
- Earthworm castings, lava sand and other low odor organic fertilizers can be used on indoor plants.
- Use gentle organic fertilizers and earthworm castings on your bulbs, annuals and perennials.

Pest Control
- If grass is loose on top of the ground it could be a sign of grub worm damage. Treat with beneficial nematodes.
- Check removed annuals for nematodes (knots on the roots). Treat soil with bio-stimulants, molasses, compost and citrus pulp.
- Watch for aphids, scale and spider mites on your houseplants. Spray with bio-stimulants, mild soap and seaweed. As a last resort use lightweight oils.

Plant

- Shrubs and trees.
- Cool season grasses.
- Spring and summer flowering perennials. Also spring flowering annuals.
- Spring bulbs - grape hyacinths, daffodils, etc. *Note: some bulbs require chilling of up to 8 weeks before planting.*

Odds 'n Ends

- Have soils tested for soil balancing needs.
- Fill compost pile with all fallen leaves, annuals and vegetable matter. Turn compost piles.
- For winter protection mulch all bare ornamental beds.
- Add mulch to the garden. No need to cultivate once you have developed healthy soil.
- Before first frost pick tomatoes and let ripen indoors.

November

Choosing Your Christmas Tree

It's tough to decide what type of Christmas tree to choose, especially with the number of varieties that are out there, but choosing what type is easy with the right information.

When choosing cut trees, go with the freshest you can find. Look for trees without dead needles and branches that are not brittle. Noble Fir is a long-lived tree that has a beautiful bluish-green color and a great symmetrical look. If you are looking for a great tree with a lot of scent, you might want to try a Balsam Fir. It can dry out quickly, so keep the tree stand filled with water. Another one of my favorites is called Fraser Fir. It has a silver color and a lot of fragrance. Another variety you might want to try is the White Fir because it is easy to decorate due to its long branches. The Blue Spruce has dense branches, but the needles drop quickly.

When you purchase the tree, make sure you have the seller remove 1 to 2 inches off the base of the tree and put it in water as quickly as possible. A tree can drink as much as 5 to 10 quarts of water per day. Also, make sure it doesn't get direct sunlight and is away from vents, heaters and fireplaces. They are very flammable, so make sure you have a fire extinguisher close by.

Cool-Weather Flowers

With the cool weather here, most of the plants in our yard take a siesta from all that hard work they did during the summer and getting any kind of color seems to fall on the shoulders of annual plantings of seasonal flowers.

Cool-season flowers are easy and don't require nearly the work that everyone is led to believe.

First, dig out your bed at least 12 inches and add 1/2-inch of peat moss with native soil. Also, add approximately 5 pounds of rock phosphate and 5 pounds of blood meal per 100 square feet.

Second, pick out the type of flowers that you want. Some plants work better in cool weather than others, so make sure you choose wisely. Some of my favorites include:

Calendula: Try frost-tolerant kablouna mix. Pinch buds back often.

Larkspur: Direct-seed right now. They love cool weather.

Lobelia: Purchase in containers. They're easy to grow and produce vibrant blue flowers.

Nasturtiums: Sow from seeds. They thrive in unimproved soil. Grow and eat.

Pansies: They are easy to grow and love rich soil and damp conditions.

Shirley Poppies: These grow from seeds and will reward you if you plant them in rich soil.

Snapdragons: They reseed easily and become perennial in cool areas of your landscape.

Sweet peas: Deep, rich soil is essential. Spencer varieties seem to work the best.

Stock: They're very fragrant and love to be grown in pots.

Next, start sowing your seeds or transplanting your flowers. After transplanting, give them a light application of liquid seaweed or Extreme Juice for a little kick. Keep them damp and fertilize with a bi-weekly application of fish emulsion or Extreme Juice. Remember to keep them deadheaded to increase the number of blooms. As for the seeds, make sure they stay damp until they are germinated.

Remember to enjoy the season and give your garden a little extra care right now. The rewards will be seen this spring.

Easy-To-Grow Seeds

A lot of seeds are easy to grow in our southwestern gardens. One of my favorites is cosmos. Try the sensation variety. These types of flowers grow rapidly and the worse you treat them, the better they grow. I plant them and cover them with a little peat moss and water them daily to get them started. Then once they get started, I cut back on the water and don't ever fertilize them.

I also like to plant Bright Light Swiss Chard. This plant is not only great in salads but brings a lot of color to your garden. The veins of the leaves turn a pretty red, yellow and orange and will give you a lot of enjoyment during all seasons as long as they get some afternoon shade.

I also plant Shirley poppies this time of year for great color in the spring. They grow all along the back side of the header that separates the lawn from my garden. They seem to thrive on the little bit of water that blows into the garden when the sprinklers come on. These seeds are so small that you may want to mix them with a little sand to get a more even distribution.

Some more plants I like to grow are:

Radishes: Easter egg or french breakfast.

Carrots: Shorter varieties.

Broccoli: Good cold-weather plant.

Cauliflower: Likes to be planted about 1 to 1-1/2 inches apart.

Wildflower Seeds: Get these from the Desert Botanical Garden for a great spring bloom.

Alyssum: Reseeds readily and blooms practically all year round.

Frost Protection

When it gets below 32 degrees at night, it's time to start thinking about protecting your garden against frost damage. You want to protect plants such as hibiscus, natal plum, cape honeysuckle, heavenly bamboo, asparagus fern, mock orange, lantana and ficus trees.

There are several ways to protect against frost damage: Water well the night before a big frost is expected. Water puts off heat as it evaporates and cools off. Try watering at about 1 or 2 am to get the best results.

Place Christmas tree lights on your plants. The large lights work best. They put off a lot of heat and you can put them on an automatic timer.

Cover your plants with blankets, newspaper, old sheets, paper bags, burlap, etc. Don't use plastic. Try not to leave it on for more than 2 or 3 days at a time. If you do, take the protection off during the day and replace again at night.

Putting Styrofoam cups on top of your cacti or small seedlings will protect them from frost. Remember to remove them during the day.

Lanterns or 60-watt or higher shop lights left on during the night will give you great frost protection if you set them around your garden.

Try any of the above methods and you'll have beautiful plants all winter long.

Keeping Your Greens Toasty

With the cold weather arriving, it's critical to remember to protect any frost-sensitive plants and trees.

Here is a quick list of some of the plants:

> *Lantana*
> *Bougainvillea*
> *Natal Plum*
> *Citrus Trees*
> *Myoporum*

Any variety of ficus-tree species and tropical type plants such as split-leaf philodendron, tropical bird of paradise and asparagus ferns.

When covering these plants, remember to cover them so that the material touches the ground. This way you are capturing the heat that is coming up from the ground.

Some of the items you can use to protect your plants are:

> *Newspaper*
> *Sheets*
> *Blankets*
> *Cardboard Boxes*
> *Straw or leaves piled on top of the plant*

For extreme cold, try adding some Christmas tree lights or a light bulb. I have even used a Coleman lantern. Some other types of cold-weather protection you might want to try are:

Floating Row Covers
Wall-O-Water
Liquid Seaweed: Spraying this on the foliage gives you approximately 4 degrees of frost protection

I have also taken evergreen branches and draped them over the low growth of plants.

Good luck and keep those plants toasty.

Live Christmas Trees And Poinsettias

The best Christmas tree to buy is a pinus elderica or elderica pine tree, sometimes called goldwater pine. This has a nice Christmas tree form.

To pick out a good tree, look for dark green, upright candles (the tips of the branches) and even growth all the way around the tree. Check for broken branches and cracks in the root ball. Make sure roots are not coming out of the bucket.

These are very heavy trees, so make sure you have some way to move these around without damaging the root ball.

Do not bring it in your house until 10 to 15 days before Christmas. Leave it on the patio in a shaded area. Water it once a day, with 2 to 3 cups of ice cubes. Ice cubes melt very slowly and give the tree a nice, deep drink of water.

Once you move it into your house, make sure the tree is not located by any vents. Use small, low-wattage Christmas lights on it because lights have a tendency to really dry trees out. Make sure you place some type of saucer underneath it so you don't do any water damage to your floor.

After the holiday is over and you want to plant the tree, plant it in a hole no deeper than the root ball. Make sure you cut the bottom off first, then cut down the side once you put it in the hole.

Back fill with the indigenous soil and place compost 3 to 4 inches deep around the tree without touching the stem of the tree.

Water regularly about every 2 to 3 days for the first 2 to 3 weeks and then you can cut back to once a week. Deep water regularly during the spring and summer.

Do not ever fertilize with synthetic fertilizers; use only organic fertilizers on pines and junipers.

Poinsettia: It's a great time of year to have poinsettias. Here are a few tips to remember about them:

Let the first 2 inches of soil dry out between watering.

Do not mist the leaves, water directly onto the soil.

No fertilizer is required.

Make sure you remove the foil or plastic wrappers the pots come in because they need good drainage.

Do not place them close to any vents.

They like 5 to 6 hours of filtered sunlight every day.

They do well with nighttime temperatures at 50 to 60 degrees and daytime temperatures of 70 degrees or above.

If you're going to use them for cuttings, cauterize them or use a match to seal the stems so they do not continue to bleed and they will last longer.

Mini-Makeover For Your Lawn

Many folks I talk to want to do big things with their lawns and gardens, but a complete overhaul can be a daunting task. If you want to make over your garden, I recommend that you start with a small project and work your way through your to-do list.

One project I took on was a home I found in Gilbert with a gravel back yard. The home has a south-facing patio and offers no protection from the sun in the summer.

The couple that lives in the home recently moved from Washington State and wanted a lush garden during the fall, winter and spring. The homeowners hoped to grow nasturtiums, roses, larkspur and many flowers you would find in a cottage-style garden. They also wanted an area of lawn to provide a nice place for their two dogs to play.

To facilitate the transformation, I designed a small area with creative touches that will compliment the rest of the yard.

My first priority was to establish an extension from the patio to become an integral part of the back yard.

I installed an informal flagstone patio set on existing soil. (To try this at home, just plop some cement on the ground, lay a piece of flagstone on top of it, make it as level as possible and let dry.)

Later, I planted creeping thyme (greek oregano will also work) between the pieces of flagstone, which, when stepped on, will add a wonderful fragrance to the area. These plants need protection from the summer heat, so I planted three 15 gallon acacia trees around the new patio area.

For function and mood, I love bistro sets. They're great for breakfast, reading the paper or just killing time. You can find these little round tables with two chairs at places like Fry's Marketplace and home improvement stores.

To dress up the backyard, I added a wonderful birdbath from Phoenix Precast to the area. The piece adds an architectural element, gives birds a place to play and provides the homeowners a great form of pest control - birds.

My last step was to add a couple of pots filled with seasonal color. In this case, I thought we should honor the Arizona Diamondbacks for their World Series win by planting purple petunias, copper chrysanthemums and white alyssum to match D-Backs' colors.

This project cost a few hundred dollars and has created a completely separate and beautiful area for the owners to spend time in. If you'd like to transform your backyard this way, it will take you just a few hours to complete a backyard getaway.

Water Gardens

I've had a water garden for several years and have found them to be as reliable as getting turkey at a Thanksgiving meal at Mom's house. You need to consider a few things before you actually install a water garden. It is best to install it where it will get 4 to 6 hours of morning sun and shade during the afternoon because afternoon sun promotes algae growth. Place the garden away from trees that shed a lot. Leaf litter is not good for ponds. A good, clean shade tree would be a ficus.

I like to use the new Bio-Filters. These filters increase the amount of micro biotic bacteria action you find in natural ponds, which helps keep them clean (you can get these at Fry's Marketplace or at *aquascapes.com*). These filters are the newest invention to come out in the last 5 to 10 years. A pond filter and liner are an absolute necessity in today's environment. Along with the filter, use a PVC liner. The liner should be 30 to 45 millimeters thick and preferably textured. The texture allows more of the microbiotic action to take place in the pond. The liner is very simple to install.

The pond will need to be excavated to a depth of 3 feet. This will enable the pond to remain cooler in temperature and sustain aquatic life. Create pockets during the excavation so you can place different types of plants in the pond. The plants will help stabilize aquatic life and take care of algae in the pond. In the pockets, place a mixture of kitty litter and peat moss to assist in stabilizing the plants. Aquatic plants are easy to grow and will help the pond stay clean.

Once the pond has been excavated and the filter, PVC and liner are in place, add river rock. Place the river rock on top of the liner and along the ledges to protect if from Arizona's intense UV sunlight. You will want to use river rock because gravel might poke holes in the liner (you can get river rock at any local rock yard). You will find the liner will last longer, plus the river rock allows beneficial bacteria to grow.

If you want, you can position underwater lights for nighttime enjoyment. With lights, you can attract great insect eaters like dragonflies and toads.

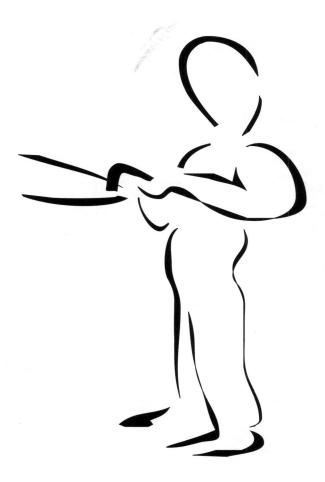

November Notes:

_____

_____

_____

_____

_____

_____

_____

_____

_____

_____

_____

_____

_____

_____

_____

_____

_____

_____

_____

_____

December
Calendar for Organic Gardening

Water
- To protect against winter cold injury, water any dry areas.

Prune
- Remove dead and damaged wood from shade trees.
- Leaving roots in the ground, cut tops off spent perennials.
- Adjust appearance of evergreens by trimming.

Fertilize
- Once or twice during winter, fertilize houseplants with earth-worm castings, lava sand, or other odorless organic fertilizers. Add 1 tbs./gal. natural apple cider vinegar.
- Lava sand, earthworm castings, and organic fertilizers are to be used for greenhouse plants.

Pest Control
- Trees with bark aphids, no treatment necessary.
- For heavy infestation of scale insects on shade and fruit trees use horticultural oil.
- Remove mistletoe from trees by removing infested limbs, if possible.
- To control scale, mealy bugs, spider mites and other insects, spray houseplants with seaweed, mild soap and biostimulants. Vinegar added to irrigation water helps also.

Plant
- Shrubs and trees.
- Spring bulbs.
- After use, plant your living Christmas trees.

Odds 'n Ends
- Turn compost piles.
- All bare soil needs mulching.
- Before first frost pick tomatoes.
- Before storing for winter, clean and oil tools.
- Run mower and trimmer engines dry of gasoline. Drain and change oil. Get repairs done before spring rush.

December

Arizona Christmas Trees

It's tough to decide what type of Christmas tree to choose, especially with the number of varieties that are out there. But choosing a Christmas tree is easy when you have the right information.

Cut Tree Characteristics:

Noble Fir: Lives the longest; branches are strong and can hold heavy ornaments; most expensive.

Grand Fir: Most fragrant; requires a lot of water; moderately priced.

Douglas Fir: Least durable; least expensive.

Cut Trees Tips:

Go with the freshest you can find. Look for trees without brittle branches or dead needles.

When purchasing a tree, ask the seller to cut off 1 to 2 inches of the base. This will allow the tree to easily absorb water.

Avoid placing your tree in direct sunlight, which will dry the tree out.

Trees are highly flammable. Keep them away from vents, heaters and fireplaces.

Keep a fire extinguisher nearby.

Cut Tree Fact:
A tree can drink as much as 5 to 10 quarts of water per day.

Live Trees for Arizona Homes:
The *Elderaca Pine/Gold Water Pine:* symmetrical; fares well in intense summer heat.

Live Tree Tips:
Try not to leave live trees in the house for more than 2 to 3 weeks. Water live trees with a couple of trays of ice cubes every day.

Planting Live Trees:
Plant live trees in wide-open areas - they can grow up to 40 feet and 60 feet high.
When planting live trees, be careful not to break the root ball.
Water the live tree often and well until it is established.

Live Tree Fact:
Pine trees are drought- and disease-tolerant and make a great addition to any landscape.

Happy Holidays!

Attracting Birds and Butterflies

Inviting birds and butterflies into your yard is an effective way of bringing another element to your landscaping and, at the same time, helping out our ecosystem. Diversity and balance are key ingredients to creating a healthy, balanced environment and without that, man has a tendency to interject synthetic solutions, such as pesticides and fertilizers. These have long-term consequences that have yet to be understood.

Often, I can drive through a neighborhood and tell what homes have used pesticides by analyzing the types and number of bird species. So, in lieu of pesticides and synthetic fertilizers, why not take a more organic approach? Start working with nature and start inviting her into your garden! A more homogenous approach is the best solution to creating healthy environments.

Birds are some of my favorite friends and to me, they add as much visual element to your garden as a beautiful waterfall. They actually will get used to it over time and become a virtual element to your life. They are great insectivores, sometimes eating their weight in insects once a week. They are constantly on watch for that pesky cricket or moth that may want to invade your garden. To attract them, put together a combination of food, water and shelter. The more you are able to emulate their natural environment, the more species you will attract.

One of the easiest ways to attract birds is with food, but there is one caveat - different types of birds like different types of food. For example, as you probably   already know, hummingbirds like nectar - a rich sugar-water in a hummingbird feeder works great for attracting them. Approximately 60 percent of their diet, however, consists of insects. So if you use insecticides, you are destroying their environment and possibly killing hummingbirds. Also, remember that if you are feeding hummingbirds with a feeder, make sure you clean out the feeder at least every three days.

The different plants that attract hummingbirds are penstemons, desert willow, wolfberry, chuparosa, ocotillo, fairy dusters, blue Palo Verdes and yellow Palo Verdes.

Other types of birds, such as quail, doves and sparrows, love to eat seeds. Mockingbirds and thrashers eat berries.

For seed-producing, try lupines, sunflowers, desert marigolds, globe mallows, brittlebushes, Palo Verdes and ironwood.

For shrubs that produce berries, try desert hackberries, barberries, wolfberries, Mexican elderberries and pyracantha.

Bare Root Fruit Trees

It's bare root season and that means one thing: You can finally plant bare root fruit trees. Before you rush out there, remember a few things:

Make sure you choose low-chill hour type of trees. Your local nursery should be able to tell you what that means, but, basically, it means trees that don't need a lot of cold weather to cause them to bear fruit.

Dig a wide, shallow hole no deeper than the root system, but 5 to 6 times the depth of the drip line of the tree. Mix in 50 percent compost and 50 percent soil, then backfill. Create a well around the tree as wide as you dug the hole and fill the well with water.

Water about every 3 to 5 days and don't let it dry out. Trim back some of the tips to an outside-facing bud eye. Ask your nursery worker for help. I don't like to trim off a lot. Make sure you purchase dwarf types of trees because full-size fruit trees are too hard to protect with blind netting during their fruiting period and, trust me, the birds will come.

A couple of combinations you might want to try are:

Apricots: I like the Blenheim (Royal) and Gold Kist. They need two types of trees to get plenty of fruit. *Hint: I treat the soil underneath my apricots with dry grass clippings for better results.*

Plums: Try Santa Rosa, Red Beauty or Laroda. They like to have nasturtiums and garlic planted at their feet.

Apples: I have great success with apples. I plant Anna's and Golden Dorett and get more apples than I can use. Plant artemisia and nasturtiums in among your apple orchard.

Peaches: Desert Gold is my favorite. Be prepared, they need a lot of pruning this time of year, but you can always make bentwood trellis, arbor, gates and fences out of the branches.

Bare-Root Roses

It's time to start buying and planting bare-root roses. These types of roses are not only beautiful, but they're inexpensive and easy to grow.

Roses come in grades of 1, 1-1/2 and 2. The grades are based on age, 2 being the youngest. I only buy grade 1 rose bushes; they tend to be heartier and survive the summer heat better. Grade 1's are usually 2 to 3 years old, and have at least 2 to 4 strong, healthy canes. Bare-root roses that have spindly canes or roots or have started to leaf out will have less chance of survival.

When choosing a plant, try to make sure the bark on the cane is plump and green. Do not purchase roses that have been dipped in wax - this can cause burns on the roses in the summer.

Here is a list of some of the best types of bare-root roses:

Don Juan: red, blooms in the second year

Gene Borner: pink, can be grown as a shrub

Showbiz: red, easy to grow (requires very little work)

Mr. Lincoln: large, red, easy to grow in the valley

Chrysler Imperial: red, a hybrid tea-style plant

Margo Koster: light pinkish tone, produces small roses

To plump up the roots and canes, soak the rose bush in a bucket of water and a capful of liquid seaweed for 12 to 24 hours before planting.

When choosing a location for your plants, try to plant them on the east side of your home where they can receive morning sun.

Plant each rose bush 3 to 4 feet apart in a location with at least 6 hours of sun a day.

To plant your rose bushes, dig a hole at least 18 inches deep by 18 inches wide. Fill the hole 1/2 full with water, and make sure it drains at the rate of at least 1 inch per hour.

In the center of the planting hole, add 1 to 2 cups soft phosphate, 1 cup soil sulfur, 1 cup gypsum and 1/2 cup rock phosphate and Texas Greensand to the bottom of the cone. Using two shovels of soil, mix the phosphate mixture into the soil and dig a cone shape into the ground. Face the bud union (looks like a knob) to the east. Remove the packing sawdust and trim any broken roots. Spread the rose's roots over the cone and backfill with a 50/50 mix of soil and compost. Keep the bud union about 2 inches above the final grade.

Water your roses slowly and deeply to keep the plant from drying out and prevent air pockets. If the rose seems to settle too deeply, gently lift the plant and add more of the 50/50 mixture; continue to water.

Water your roses at least every other day for the first 2 weeks. To protect the canes from drying out cover them with straw or moist peat moss; remove covering when new growth shows.

Note: Roses love companion plants like garlic, artemisia, day lilies and moss rose.

Hint: Remember to fertilize regularly.

Gardening In Cold Weather

There are a lot of reasons not to grow a garden during the winter, but growing a garden in the winter is not as hard as the experts would like us to believe.

You must first put in the right types of plants. Try growing carrots, broccoli, brussel sprouts, sweet peas and lettuce like Black Simpson and Red Sails.

The best way is to try to purchase the vegetables from a nursery in six-pack containers. Then, install them against a south facing wall, which captures the most heat from the sun. You can also try to get these types of plants to germinate from seeds. If you choose to plant them from seed, dig a trench in well prepared soil. The trench should be covered with clear plastic. This system keeps the soil warmer and the humidity higher, which allows better growing conditions.

Along with this, I have built mini greenhouses out of PVC pipe and plastic to create warmer conditions for my winter crops. I find I get the most tender and sweetest crops during the winter.

Growing Plants For Free

Believe it or not, you can produce plants from just your trimmings, or for that matter, from your neighbors' trimmings. In my world, it's called propagation. It's been used for ages as a way to reproduce plant material from a parent plant. So when you make a cutting, make sure you like what you see. Unlike seeds, cuttings allow you to exactly reproduce the parent and retain the improved qualities of the cultivars. I have experimented with this technique for more than 20 years and have had great success with a few of the following trees and shrubs:

Trees:
Ironwood
Plumeria: You can purchase cuttings from Hawaii.
Mesquite: This is an important way of producing thornless varieties.
Cottonwood or any of the poplar species.
Mimosa
Orchid Tree: Try the Hong Kong variety for its great blooming period.
Ficus Trees
RubberTrees

Shrubs:
Bush Bougainvillea: This is one of the easiest plants to propagate from
  cuttings. Protect from frost.
Aloe: It's a great plant with healing powers.
Four-Wing Saltbush: This is good fire retardant and it attracts native birds.
Fairydusters: A great accent plant that attracts hummingbirds.
Leucophyllum or Sage: Flowers great if not sheared back.
Pineapple Guava: This is a great slow-growing, fruit-producing plant.
Rose

Ground Cover:
Australian saltbush
Dark saltbush
Ice plant
Dalea Greggii Dwarf Indigo Bush: This is one of my favorite ground
  covers.

Vines:
Campisis Radicans: Common trumpet creeper.

Cactus:
Prickly Pear
Ocotillo: Water occasionally until new leaves appear.
Pencil Tree and most *Euphorbia* species.

There are a lot more species of plants that can be reproduced from the cuttings. It's not difficult to do. Follow these basic steps:

Make your cuttings. Most cuttings come from what we call softwood. This is the tip of the plant and should be no longer than 2 inches long. The cuttings should represent new growth and should be fairly limber.

Prune off any new leaves that will go below the soil line. I also cut any leaves that are exposed above the soil line by half to slow down water loss.

Deeply and thoroughly cover any wounds with rooting hormone (or your own saliva works just as well). This can be purchased from any local nursery. It has a shelf life so make sure it is fresh.

Install the cutting into a small container of well-drained soil made up of 1/2 perlite and 1/2 peat moss.

Install the cutting into a Ziploc bag to act as a mini greenhouse. This also creates a higher humidity level, which helps with faster rooting. Make sure to use some small pencils to prop the bags up so they do not rest on the plant.

Place the plant in an east-facing window and check it every 2 to 3 weeks for root growth.

Once the plant is rooted, you can transplant it into a larger container made up of regular potting soil. You will have to experiment a little and will not have 100 percent success, but the rewards are great, especially when you say "I grew it for free".

Healing Herbs

With the upcoming cold and flu season, it is easy to forget that running down to our local drug store is not our only option. For centuries, our ancestors have used herbs as a source of vitamins and medicines in healing ailments. In fact, herbs are still used to a great extent in Europe and Asia.

Without getting into the political ramifications, calling yourself an herbalist here in the United States is illegal. However, using many of the herbs that do a great job of healing is not and you can grow many of these things right in your own backyard.

Over the years, I have had my best success growing many of my herbs in 1 or 5 gallon plastic buckets. Many nurseries will be glad to give the buckets to you or may charge a small fee. During the winter, I like to set them in full sun and during the spring, summer and fall, setting them in an eastern early morning exposure to the sun is best. You might also want to wrap them in some aluminum foil to reflect some of the heat that the black buckets have a tendency to absorb during warm periods.

Herbs are not a high fertilizer consumer but a light dose of fish emulsion every 2 to 3 weeks doesn't hurt. Also, make sure to flush the salts out of the bucket every time you water with a good soaking of the plant medium every 1 to 2 weeks. This is just a matter of watering until you see moisture running out of the holes in the bottom of the bucket.

There are many types of herbs that help with different maladies. Here are a few of my favorites:

Garlic: It's easy to grow, especially around roses to prevent insect infestation. I also use the raw garlic juice from the crushed cloves mixed with hot water and honey for a sore throat and cold remedy. You can also eat raw garlic to fight bronchial infections.

Dandelions: Don't throw them away. The leaves are a rich source of vitamins and the root is a mild laxative.

Peppermint: You can grow peppermint in early morning shade. Tea can be made from the dried leaves to help soothe coughs.

Rosemary: I grow this around my home as an insect barrier and its flowers and leaves are good for colds and indigestion.

Sage: Tea is made from the leaves to cure indigestion and helps to fight cold symptoms.

Onions: I will place slices of onions on insect bites. Crushed leaves of lemon balm will also help.

Calendula Petals: Steep petals in hot boiling water until soft. Squeeze the petals and apply as a compress to treat minor cuts and burns.

Parsley: Tea has been used to treat high blood pressure, heart failure and allergies.

And for the New Year's hangover, steep peppermint and thyme leaves in a cup of boiling water, strain and sip. If the headache persists, try a small leaf of feverfew between 2 pieces of bread for quick relief.

If you're taking other medications, or if you're pregnant, make sure you contact your doctor before taking these remedies.

Home Grown Houseplants

I'm sure most of you have thrown out those avocado pits, pineapple tops and citrus seeds, but believe it or not, all of them make wonderful houseplants that give you years of enjoyment and, best of all, they're free and easy to grow.

When I was growing up in Hawaii, I was always intrigued with pineapples.

Until approximately 10 years ago, I had never met anyone who could grow them successfully in the valley, but believe it or not, they're easy. When you purchase a pineapple, cut off the crown with approximately 1 inch of the rind still attached. Dry it for 24 to 36 hours and then root it in well-drained soil.

This soil consists of:

> *1 part Perlite*
> *1 part peat moss*
> *1 part compost*

When growing your *pineapple*, you need to spray it with fish emulsion approximately 2 times a month because it takes in nutrients through its leaves. Keep the soil moist but not soggy and give it a minimum of 3 to 4 hours of sun per day. You can also grow it as an office plant under fluorescent lights.

Maintain a temperature around 70 to 80 degrees and wait about 2 years. If you don't see a fruit develop, enclose it in a plastic bag with an apple. The apple releases ethylene gas, which is used for stimulating fruit production.

Why save *citrus seeds*? Because they will produce small citrus bushes. As you might already know, citrus is meant to be trimmed like a bush.

Soak the seeds for 12 hours in lukewarm water and then place them pointed end-up in all-purpose potting soil approximately 1/4-inch deep.

Keep the soil moist and place them in a dark room until they sprout. Make sure the room stays approximately 70 to 80 degrees. After they sprout, make sure to thin them out or transplant them into a separate, slightly larger pot. Be sure to let them dry between watering. Remember, citrus like a fairly dry environment, so keep them away from moisture.

The next time you spit out those *grape* seeds, make sure you do it into a 5 inch pot with a good all-purpose potting soil. They need to be planted approximately 2 to 3 times the diameter of the seed because they grow aggressively. Grapes love light, so locating the pot near a hot southern window is ideal. They're hardy and take an occasional dose of fish emulsion and like to dry out between watering.

The next time you purchase *carrots*, don't throw away the foliage. Cut off the tops and leave approximately 1 inch of the root attached. Cut back the foliage, leaving 1 to 2 inches of the leaves. Snuggle the root into a bowl of water with some pebbles and you're on your way to great little houseplant. You can also do this with *beets* and *turnip greens*.

Plants For Christmas Decorating

Here are some tips for taking care of holiday plants:

Poinsettias:

Need 6 to 8 hours of filtered to full sunlight a day.

Don't like to be moved.

Prefer to be cooler at night (50 to 60 degrees) and warmer during the day (70 to 80 degrees). A western exposure works great.

In the cooler months, they can be outside; during warmer months, they can be inside.

They are susceptible to frost damage.

Take the foil wrap off of them because they don't like their roots to be wet.

If you're going to use them for cutting, be sure you burn or cauterize the tips so the sap won't run out and they will last longer.

They like to be moist but not wet. Let them dry out to the touch on top before watering every 3 to 5 days.

Cyclamen:

They like to be moist.

They are great Christmas plants.

Place in a tray of water with pebbles underneath it.

Like full to filtered sun.

Like to be in a cool location.

They may go dormant during the summer. You can re-pot them in the fall.

Christmas Cactus:

This plant likes to be on the dry side. Water every 5 to 10 days. Let them dry out between watering.

It should remain in one location.

Needs acid-type soil. Try to water with 1 tbsp. vinegar per 1 gallon of water every time you water.

Fertilize with small amounts of Extreme Juice.

It transplants easily.

The Bare Bones About Bare Root

Bare root fruit and nut trees do very well in this region. Apples, guavas, oranges, blackberries and pecans thrive in the desert and bring diversity to your garden.

To produce fruit, deciduous fruits and nuts have minimum low-temperature requirements. When it gets down to 45 degrees or below for 60 minutes, you've got yourself a "chill hour." Different types of trees have different chill-hour requirements. Choose varieties with low minimums, usually 250 chill hours or less. Maricopa County usually has 300 to 400 chill hours per year.

To develop strong trees with healthy fruit, I'm going to let you in on a couple of secrets (although these secrets don't apply to citrus). First, the earlier in the season you plant, the better chance your tree has for success. Second, different areas of your yard has different temperatures. Some are cooler, while some are warmer.

Cold air is heavy and lingers in low spots. Fruit and nut trees like the coolest part of the yard. Seek the lowest part of the yard, with eastern or northeastern exposure. Better yet, dig out and lower a portion of the yard, near a solid block wall, which is ideal for collecting cold air. This also helps channel water and rain to the trees for irrigation purposes.

Buy and plant bare root plants as soon as possible, up until early February. The sooner they are in, the better they grow. However, you can install container-grown plants until mid-March. It's usually too hot after that.

If any of your fences have drainage holes, sometimes called "wagon wheels" for their shape at the bottom of block fences, close them off when it's not raining with a board or even newspaper.

Some trees will do better in higher elevations, because of their chill-hour requirements. Within the Salt River Valley, elevations range from about 1,100 feet in Phoenix to 1,800 feet near Apache Junction, while parts of Cave Creek and Carefree are up to 2,500 feet.

In general, planting rules include digging a hole no deeper than the root system and no wider than 5 to 6 times the width of the roots. Fill the planting hole with several inches of water the day before and make sure all the water drains entirely away. Back-fill the hole with native soil mixed with organic material, Texas Greensand and lavasand, and build a berm around the tree to hold water in.

Most of the fruit and nut trees are deciduous. They drop their leaves in the fall and go dormant in winter. They should be planted on the eastern side of the yard to provide cool shade in the summer and warm sun through in the winter. If you plant well and care for trees organically they can live from 10 to 15 years.

Dave's Favorite Products

I mention my favorite products several times in the pages beforehand, so I wanted to provide you with descriptions of each product. These are all organic products, and are sold at Poco Verde Landscape, located at 520 W. Warner Rd., Tempe, Arizona. Phone is 480-893-3948, or on my website, *www.gardenguy.com*.

6-2-2 SOIL FOOD

Great fertilizer for vegetable and flower gardens. Use in conjunction with a foliar feeding program. Produces outstanding growth/blooms all season.

7-2-2 SOIL FOOD

An excellent, slow release fertilizer for trees, shrubs, and other perennials. Great for spring lawn fertilization.

BAT GUANO

Excellent, natural soil conditioner. Quickly turns a brown lawn green. Enriches your garden to produce healthy plants and vegetables. Ideal for conditioning all types of garden soils. High in nitrogen.

BIOGANIC WASP & HORNET KILLER

Kills wasps, hornets and yellow jackets on contact. No pesticidal residue. Natural, active ingredients from plant oils. Environmentally friendly, effective and safe around children and pets.

BIOGANIC WEED & GRASS KILLER

Made from plant oils, such as cloves and sesame. Effective, environmentally friendly weed control. Safe around children and pets.

BORIC ACID
Easy to use powder that is odorless, non-staining. Kills roaches, waterbugs, ants and silverfish. Sprinkle around baseboards, behind sinks. Do not use outdoors (it kills plants!). Blend with sugar or peanut butter to use as a bait. Keep out of reach of children and pets.

COMPOST
Ideal for conditioning soils in flower beds, vegetable gardens, planting grass or sod, and mulching. A biologically active product that builds healthy soil and healthy plants. Increases moisture retention in the soil and makes soil easier to dig, till and weed. Use as a mulch, 4 inches thick, to retain moisture, reduce weeds and lower the temperature of the soil.

COMPOST MICROBES
Contains billions of decomposing microbes. Collected from compost piles. Just a handful accelerates the decomposition of composting material. Also, an excellent spot treatment for brown patches and other fungus in lawns.

CROPGUARD
Made from Yucca, Agave and other natural extracts. Safe/Organic. Repellant to small body insects such as aphids. Indoor/Outdoor, although strong garlic odor.

DIATOMACEOUS EARTH
Targets all crawling pests, including ants, crickets, roaches, fleas and ticks. Odorless, non-toxic, fine powder. Dust your entire yard, house, even pets.

EARTH WORM CASTINGS
Rich in nutrients, increases tilth and friability and aeration of the soil. Great to use in any type of soil.

EXTREME JUICE
The Garden Guy's own blend of fish emulsion, liquid seaweed, humic acid, soft phosphate and much more. An all organic product that "makes things grow". Concentrated fertilizer.

LIQUID SEAWEED
Great fertilizer that you can use to foliar feed.

MOLASSES
Increases microbiotic activity in soil, also reduces fishy odor when using fish emulsion.

ROCK PHOSPHATE
Great non-burning source of phosphorus. Place in hole at time of planting seeds or transplants. Promotes seed germination, root growth and flower blossoms.

ROCKET FUEL
Great fertilizer for seedlings and transplants. Fourteen unique organic ingredients. Specifically formulated for young roots and gets plants off to a great start.

SEA TEA
Ideal for all vegetables and leafy plants. Increases plant growth.

SHAKE AWAY - DEER
Powdered coyote urine to repel deer. Non-toxic around pets, humans and environment. Sprinkle along perimeter of lawn, flower-beds or wherever needed in yard.

SHAKE AWAY - RABBITS
Powdered fox urine to repel rabbits. Non-toxic around pets, humans and environment. Sprinkle along perimeter of lawn, flower-beds or wherever needed in your yard.

TEXAS GREENSAND
A naturally occurring mineral called glauconite. A rich source of iron and other minerals. Excellent soil conditioner for lawn and garden. Dry and spreadable. Contains manganese which is needed for keeping queen palms healthy.

VOLCANITE
Paramagnetic Greensand, lava sand, basalt and zeolite. Paramagnetism is a low-level energy source. Increases plant growth. By 20 to 30 percent and reduces water needs.

Product Notes:

_____
_____
_____
_____
_____
_____
_____
_____
_____
_____
_____
_____
_____
_____
_____
_____
_____
_____
_____
_____
_____

Notes:

Notes:

Notes:

Notes:

Notes:

Notes:

Notes:

Notes:

Notes:

Notes:

Notes:

Notes:

Notes:

Notes:

Notes:

Notes:

Notes:

Notes: